D1123630

Women in Love

A Novel of Mythic Realism

TWAYNE'S MASTERWORK STUDIES

Robert Lecker, General Editor

Women in Love

A Novel of Mythic Realism

Charles L. Ross

Twayne Publishers • Boston
A Division of G.K. Hall & Co.

Women in Love: A Novel of Mythic Realism
Charles L. Ross

Twayne's Masterwork Studies No. 65
Copyright 1991 by G.K. Hall & Co.
All rights reserved.
Published by Twayne Publishers
A division of G.K. Hall & Co.
70 Lincoln Street
Boston, Massachusetts 02111

Copyediting supervised by Barbara Sutton
Book production by Gabrielle B. McDonald
Book design by Barbara Anderson
Typeset in Sabon with Aldus display type
by Worldcomp of Sterling, Virginia

10 9 8 7 6 5 4 3 2 1 (hc.)
10 9 8 7 6 5 4 3 2 1 (pb.)

Library of Congress Cataloging-in-Publication Data

Ross, Charles L., 1945–
    Women in love : a novel of mythic realism / Charles L. Ross.
        p.   cm.—(Twayne's masterwork studies ; 65)
    Includes bibliographical references and index.
        ISBN 0-8057-8057-2 (alk. paper).—ISBN 0-8057-8106-4 (pbk.: alk.
    paper)
        1. Lawrence, D. H. (David Herbert), 1885–1930. Women in love.
    I. Title. II. Series.
    PR6023.A93W657   1991
    823'.912—dc20   90-48716
                                                              CIP

Contents

CONTENTS

Note on the References and Acknowledgments

Women in Love is cited in my annotated edition, published by Penguin in the English Library series (1982) and currently reprinted in Penguin Classics. This edition is based on the text in the first, privately printed Seltzer edition (1920).

The titles of the twin novels, *The Rainbow* and *Women in Love*, remained fluid during six years of writing. "The Sisters" or the "Brangwensaga" were synonymous names for the project as a whole in its many versions. "Sisters" is the title of the first chapter in *Women in Love*. *Sisters* is also the title of a forthcoming edition of the penultimate version of *Women in Love*, announced by Cambridge University Press; it has been adopted here to clarify references to Lawrence's manuscript revisions of *Women in Love*.

In transcribing revisions from the manuscripts I have used square brackets [ ] for deleted material and pointed brackets < > for substitutions, which are placed directly after what they replace or where they were inserted.

It is a pleasure to acknowledge the financial assistance of the Guggenheim Foundation, the National Endowment for the Humanities, and the University of Hartford. I am indebted to the Harry Ransom Humanities Research Center at the University of Texas for permission to consult Lawrence's manuscripts. Gerald Pollinger, acting for the Estate of Frieda Lawrence Ravagli, has permitted quotation from Lawrence's published and unpublished works. Richard Ross, Paul Smith, and Enid Stubin gave me the benefit of careful readings. This book is dedicated to my wife, Barbara, and our daughters, Anna, Fionnuala, and Charlotte, for their encouragement and love.

D.H. Lawrence

Chronology: D. H. Lawrence's Life and Works

1885   David Herbert Lawrence born 11 September in Eastwood, Nottinghamshire, to Arthur Lawrence and Lydia Beardsall, the fourth of five children and third of three boys.

1901   Death of older brother, William Ernest Lawrence, the firstborn son, who appears as William in *Sons and Lovers*. Lawrence meets Jessie Chambers, "Miriam" in the novel. Goes to work for a firm manufacturing surgical appliances.

1902   Accepts position as teacher in Eastwood.

1906   Enters teacher-training course offered at University College, Nottingham. Begins first novel, *The White Peacock*.

1907   Publishes first story, "A Prelude," in *Nottinghamshire Guardian*.

1908   Awarded teacher's certificate by University College. Goes to teach at Davidson Road School, Croydon, South London.

1909   Jessie Chambers chooses, copies, and submits two early poems to *The English Review*. The editor, Ford Madox Hueffer (later Ford), publishes "Dreams Old and Nascent" and "Baby Movements." Becomes romantically interested in fellow teacher, Helen Corke, whose personal history and notes provide material for second novel, *The Trespasser*.

1910   Begins *The Trespasser*. Works on a "colliery" novel called "Paul Morel" (later *Sons and Lovers*). Engaged briefly to Louisa (Louie) Burrows. Mrs. Lawrence, ill with cancer, dies on 9 December.

1911   *The White Peacock* published in January. Falls ill with pneumonia in November and stops teaching.

1912   Publishes *The Trespasser*. Resigns teaching post; returns home; attends classes at University College. Falls in love with Frieda von Richthofen Weekley, wife of French professor, daughter of a German baron, and mother of two children. In May they elope to Germany and Italy. Lawrence carries manuscript of *Sons and Lovers* with him. Revises novel and writes many of the poems later published in *Look! We Have Come Through!*

1913   Publishes *Love Poems and Others* and *Sons and Lovers*. Writes travel sketches, revised in 1915 and published as *Twilight in Italy*. Writes early versions of "The Sisters" in Italy.

1914   Submits a version of *The Rainbow* to publisher. It is rejected as too sexually explicit. Marries Frieda in July. World War I declared in August. Rewrites and publishes early stories in *The Prussian Officer and Other Stories*. Writes but does not publish *Study of Thomas Hardy*. Begins final rewriting of *The Rainbow*.

1915   *The Rainbow* published, suppressed, and burned by court order. Lawrences move to Cornwall, having failed to secure passports for America. They are trapped in England for the rest of the war.

1916   *Twilight in Italy* and *Amores* published. Begins writing "The Sisters" again, eventually to become *Women in Love*.

1917   Fails medical examination for military service. Suspected of spying for Germany and expelled from Cornwall. Rewrites *Women in Love* for "the unseen witnesses." Composes early versions of essays on American literature, later rewritten and published as *Studies in Classic American Literature*.

1918   Writes first version of *The Fox*.

1919   Falls ill with influenza. Puts finishing touches to *Women in Love* and writes foreword to novel for American readers (published posthumously). Leaves England for Europe, never again to live in his native land.

1920   Living in Italy and writing poems later published in *Birds, Beasts and Flowers* and another version of American literature essays. Publishes *The Lost Girl*.

1921   Visits Sardinia and writes *Sea and Sardinia*. Publishes *Psychoanalysis and the Unconscious* and lengthens *The Fox* by adding a "strange and fiery brush."

1922   Publishes *Aaron's Rod*, *Fantasia of the Unconscious*, and *England, My England*. Travels to Australia via Ceylon. Works on *Kangaroo*. Leaves for Taos, New Mexico.

1923   Publishes final version of *Studies in Classic American Litera-*

Chronology: D.H. Lawrence's Life and Works

	ture. Travels to Mexico City and Lake Chapala. Begins "Quetzalcoatl" (later *The Plumed Serpent*).
1924	Travels to England; returns to Mexico via France, Germany, and Taos. Writes *St. Mawr*. Death of his father.
1925	Ill with malaria in Mexico. Finishes *The Plumed Serpent* while recuperating in Taos. Returns to England and Europe with Frieda. His illness diagnosed as tuberculosis.
1926	Settles outside Florence at the Villa Mirenda, where he writes two versions of *Lady Chatterley's Lover*. Begins painting "seriously, on my own," not just copying as in his youth.
1927	Paints, visits Etruscan tombs and archaeological museums in Italy, begins *Etruscan Places*. Rewrites early poetry for *Collected Poems*. Publishes *Mornings in Mexico*.
1928	Publishes third version of *Lady Chatterley's Lover*. Lives in south of France, where manuscript of *Pansies* is seized by postal authorities. Writes "Introduction to These Paintings."
1929	Paintings displayed at Warren Gallery in London and seized by police in July. Writes *Apocalypse* and *Last Poems*, both published posthumously.
1930	Dies of tuberculosis in Vence, France, on 2 March.
1935	Body exhumed, cremated, and buried in a shrine on his ranch in Taos, New Mexico.

Literary and Historical Context

1

Composition

D.H. Lawrence was born in 1885 and grew up in the Midlands of England, the birthplace of the Industrial Revolution. His father, a coal miner, and his mother, the daughter of an engineer and preacher, created a household that contained tensions between working-class and bourgeois culture, vernacular and the King's English, common knowledge and book learning, rootedness and aspiration to a world beyond. Lawrence's hometown of Eastwood is near the city of Nottingham and also on the edge of Sherwood Forest, and what the English critic Raymond Williams calls a "border" sensibility is reflected in Lawrence's work. Magical evocations of nature are juxtaposed with pictures of encroaching industry, and the life of the body is often hampered by the rigidities of social class. In part because Mrs. Lawrence refused to let her sons follow their father down the pit, Lawrence became a scholarship boy and climbed out of the working class, though at the cost of lifelong feelings of alienation and guilt. The native never returned to the darkly passionate, violent working-class life of the Midlands, but he never stopped loving, hating, and imaginatively re-creating it. The story of his growing up and leaving native ground is re-created superbly in *Sons and Lovers* (1913). There and in *D. H.*

Lawrence: A Personal Record by Jessie Chambers, Lawrence's first love and the model for Miriam Leivers in *Sons and Lovers,* we may read of the active intellectual life young Lawrence pursued amid what F. R. Leavis called "the apparent disadvantages" of "an ugly mining village in the spoilt Midlands."[1] One of Lawrence's distinctions is to have risen through the obdurate English class system and achieved a career of world significance.

Lawrence became a schoolteacher in London (1908–11), writing novels, poems, and stories and, through the initiative of Jessie Chambers, coming to the attention of Ford Madox Ford, editor of the famous *English Review.* To have a woman supporting his career was a condition that Lawrence later claimed to be an artistic necessity: "a woman that I love sort of keeps me in direct communication with the unknown."[2] Then in 1912 he fell in love with the wife of his French professor at University College, Nottingham. He eloped with her to Europe and a life of wandering and living by his pen. The woman was Frieda von Richthofen Weekley, daughter of a baron in the Prussian army and the formidable presence behind Lawrence's extraordinary portraits of women. He and Frieda created a marriage that, for all its turbulence, was the source of some of the greatest fiction in the language on the subject of married love.

Lawrence carried the manuscript of *Sons and Lovers* to Europe and, while contending with her husband and parents for Frieda's affections, "slaved" at rewriting the novel whose protagonist he had outgrown and come to "*loathe.*"[3] The writing of *Sons and Lovers* was partly therapeutic: "one sheds one's sicknesses in books—repeats and presents again one's emotions, to be master of them."[4] Nevertheless, the conflict between class consciousness and natural sexual instinct reappears throughout his writings. The puritanical mother in *Sons and Lovers,* though seduced by the miner's sensual "flame," is dismayed by his lack of intellectual curiosity and, in recoil, preserves her superiority by belittling and finally breaking his manhood. The father has not only physical grace and sexual vigor but also natural charm and manners, all of which are brutalized by his own temper, the industrial system, and the family's hostility. Their parental legacy to Paul Morel, the protagonist, is suppression or deflection of the natural self. In one conversation with his mother, with whom he always sides, Paul voices a rare sympathy for his father's life: "I belong to the common people ... from the middle classes one gets ideas, and from the common people—life itself." But his mother accuses him of reverse snobbery, asking a question Lawrence could never answer: "It's all very well, my boy. But, then, why don't you go and talk to your father's pals?"[5] Despite all the shortcomings of the Morel marriage, its snobbery and brutality, it does contain the true passion needed for individual growth: "That's what one *must have* ... the real, real flame of feeling through another person—once, only once, if it only lasts three months. See, my mother looks as if she's *had* everything that was necessary for her living and developing."[6] Here Lawrence implies the future course of his fiction, the depiction of passion as a force of renovation, to be celebrated even when it disrupts conventional social arrangements such as bourgeois marriage.

In his youthful love for Miriam, Paul is torn between spirituality and sexuality and then, in the first love of manhood with Clara Dawes, between sexuality and individuality. As Clara wonders, "But is it *me* you want or is it *It?*"[7] The "immensity of passion" Paul experiences with Clara not only expresses his sexual nature but puts him in touch with the "Beyond" in moments when the language foreshadows the idiom of *The Rainbow:* "They had met, and included in their meeting the thrust of the manifold grass-stems, the cry of the peewit, the wheel of the stars."[8] Yet Paul makes excessive demands on sexuality because, after the loss of his mother and estrangement from the working class, he finds no mediating institutions through which to express his full self—sexual, artistic, and social. At the equivocal ending of the novel, Paul walks companionless but "quickly" across the dark fields and toward the "glowing town." It is a characteristically Lawrentian moment of fictional closure, leaving open the possibility that Paul and, subsequently, Ursula will find a companion and a way through society to what the Brangwens call the "beyond."

Between 1913 and 1919 Lawrence's imaginative energy was mainly channeled into a long novel given the working title "The Sisters." Its evolution through many drafts and publication as two novels, *The Rainbow* and *Women in Love,* make a fascinating story.[9] Lawrence tackled "*the* problem of today, the establishment of a new relation, or the readjustment of the old one, between man and woman."[10] Hence the seminal theme of both novels was "woman becoming individual, self-responsible, taking her own initiative."[11]

A surviving fragment of an early draft suggests that "The Sisters" began with a plot for *Women in Love* and that Lawrence then proceeded backwards in fictional time, writing *The Rainbow* before embarking again on *Women in Love.* It is a scene between Gudrun, Gerald, and Loerke. After weeks of vacillation, Gerald has made up his mind to marry Gudrun, who is pregnant with his child. Meanwhile, humiliated and desperate, Gudrun has turned to Loerke, a German sculptor, as a possible father for the child. Loerke is with her when Gerald arrives to propose. Stunned by her passionate resentment, Gerald can muster only the lame excuse that he didn't "know"—of his love for her? of her pregnancy? The competition between Gerald and Loerke for the silent woman mounts until Gerald threatens the sculptor and then subsides in shame. Realizing Gudrun has chosen Gerald, Loerke leaves. Gerald's cry of shame moves Gudrun, although his actions have killed much of her love for him. The fragment ends on a note of ambiguous resolution as Gerald vows to himself that he will submit to suffering and win Gudrun's love. That Gudrun might become pregnant with Gerald's child was a possibility that Lawrence entertained for the end of "The Sisters" as late as the penultimate version of *Women in Love* in 1916.

The Rainbow was published in September 1915 and suppressed as obscene by the police in November. Although Lawrence had reluctantly censored the proofs, the novel still proved too candid—"a monotonous wilderness of phallicism," according to one reviewer.[12] More than a thousand copies were seized and burned. Denied permission to leave for America, Lawrence became an exile in his own country, moving from

London to Land's End in Cornwall. In the next few years he and Frieda were reduced to the condition of virtual beggary, just at the time he was writing his greatest novel. Finished in 1917, *Women in Love* had to wait until 1920 before it was published privately in New York.

Although the fictional time is prewar (roughly 1912) and the war is alluded to only twice, *Women in Love* may be said to have an allegorical dimension that is antiwar. Like other major innovators of modern literature—Yeats, Woolf, Pound, Eliot, and Joyce—Lawrence did not serve in the war. But he had lived in Germany and Italy on the eve of war. Moreover, as he explained in a letter to the American poet Harriet Monroe, the noncombatant artist could still fight: "It is the business of the artist to follow [the war] home to the heart of the individual fighters . . . it's at the bottom of almost every Englishman's heart . . . the *will* to war."[13] *Women in Love* indirectly reflects the bitterness of the war in the fiercely aggressive, even murderous interpersonal actions of Birkin and Hermione or Gerald and Gudrun, in Gerald's reorganization of the mines and his defense of nationalism, and in Birkin's opposition to an ideology of industrial development that exalts the "pure instrumentality" of the machine—a machine that grinds up the spirit of the workers as surely as the military machine across the channel was devouring soldiers.

The novel is also postwar in the sense that it reflects the passion for traveling and for departures made possible by advances in technology and transportation accelerated by the war. Gerald Crich is a modern hero who, like postwar Europeans in general, "began to pedal, swim, ski, and scramble up the sides of mountains."[14] Indeed, *Women in Love* might be said to debunk in advance this naive myth of progress through technological advance or sheer movement. The postwar desire to travel for spiritual nourishment or rebirth can be traced to the war generation's feeling of being "wanderers between two worlds."[15] *Women in Love* contains a dialectical representation of this desire. Birkin both participates in and criticizes the desire to "hop off" the known world; in the end, he admits that travel is not a "way out" so much as a "way in" again and that it is delusional to pursue life as "a picaresque novel." Lawrence, like Birkin, was "damned and doomed to the old effort at serious living" (383), the effort to bridge the abyss with new human and social structures. His famous circumnavigation of the globe was not escapism but a search for an audience and a society that might nurture new forms of relationship between individuals. That he never found such a place—except in the imaginative reconstructions or utopian projections of Australia, Mexico, the American Southwest, and Italy—or that he added the postscript "This place no good" to one of his last letters, is not an admission of defeat but the record of an undaunted thought adventurer. Lawrence's imaginative reports from cultural borderlines are searching self-criticisms of a representative artist.

Though written in internal exile, *Women in Love* is European in scope. Lawrence judged the novel genre superior to all other forms of knowledge because it is "the highest example of subtle inter-relatedness that man has discovered."[16] Science, philosophy, and religion have mastered "different bits of man alive," but unlike the novel they "never get the whole hog."[17] *Women in Love* makes extraordinary efforts to reflect the spirit of the age. It is a novel of ideas in which characters debate the politics of industrialism and nationalism, historical progress or decline, modern painting, modernist architecture, and the aesthetics of art. Its structure reveals the influence of Greek tragedy and foreshadows the cinematic techniques of postmodernist fiction. Its use of anthropology and mythology places it in the company of modernist works by Conrad and Joyce and T. S. Eliot that create artistic unity in a world grown so complex as to appear anarchic.

Lawrence mixes different sorts of discourse within a realistic fiction: travelogue, philosophical treatise, and mythological speculation. Yet as a superb practitioner of each of these genres, in such books as *Twilight in Italy, Fantasia of the Unconscious,* and *Apocalypse,* he knew that the novelist must preserve the "trembling instability of the balance" and avoid the "absolute." Hence this "bright book of life," as he called the genre of the novel, contains under powerful control many of the intellectual and emotional trends that we identify as modern.

2

The Importance of the Work

The Rainbow and *Women in Love* are really an organic artistic
whole.[1]

Any novel exists in a web of meanings whose strands are biography,
history, and other works of fiction. This truth about literary creativity
is more evident than usual in D. H. Lawrence's practice. The reader of
Women in Love who has previously read *The Rainbow* and recognizes
references to Ursula Brangwen's childhood in Cossethay, the Marsh
farm, Tilly the servant, and Anton Skrebensky or who learns that
Lawrence wrote "Vol. I" on the last page of the manuscript of *The
Rainbow* and referred to *Women in Love* as a "potential sequel" may
be surprised to learn that many critics assert the separation of these
twin novels. For example, F. R. Leavis, having declared the lack of
"organic connexion" or "any continuity" between the books, calls the
last chapter of *The Rainbow* "not an end but a cessation" and "an
arbitrary formal 'Finis.'"[2] As Lawrence himself asserted, however, the
two novels form an artistic whole, twins bound together in familial
though paradoxical relationship. This second volume of what Lawrence called a "Brangwensaga" continues the bildungsroman of Ursula

9

Brangwen that occupies the last half of *The Rainbow*. Severing one twin from the other has prevented full comprehension of Lawrence's artistic intentions, particularly in *Women in Love*. Having both an integrity of its own and a vital link to a previous novel, *Women in Love* also illustrates an aspect of creativity. As Harold Bloom has remarked, "though a strong poem is a fresh start, such a start is a starting-again."[3] Consequently, though the subject of this book is *Women in Love*, I pay due attention to its twin and, more widely, to its relationship to other works by Lawrence that it echoes, completes, or influences.

Women in Love emerged from a prolonged and complex process of writing. In a retrospective foreword Lawrence urged that the "struggle for verbal consciousness" should not be left out in art.[4] As usual he was transforming a fact of his artistic life into a theme in his fiction. The voluminous surviving manuscripts of the twin novels provide a record of inventiveness and pertinacity rarely if ever equaled in literary history. So pervasive were the revisions of *Women in Love*, for example, that an edition of the penultimate draft will be published separately under the working title Lawrence used for the twin novels and gave to the first chapter of the second, *Sisters*. Although process and finished product must not be confused, the evidence of the manuscripts often suggests interpretations. A sampling of revisions in the manuscripts of the novel gives a glimpse into the artist's workshop and counters the mistaken notion, still widespread, that Lawrence wrote too rapidly to perfect his craft.

The judgment of F. R. Leavis in 1955 remains substantially true today: "the insight, the wisdom, the revived and re-educated feeling for health, that Lawrence brings are what, as our civilization goes, we desperately need."[5] Leavis, the champion of Lawrence as "the great writer of our own phase of civilization," stressed Lawrence's critique of industrial mass society, his defense of human life in all its marvelous individuality or "disquality," and his search for a renewed, "organic" community. Leavis's judgment has been strengthened by the more recent critical emphasis on ambiguity and equivocation in Lawrence's vision of the moral life. As H. M. Daleski, Colin Clarke, Frank Kermode, and others have argued, Lawrence's representation of moral experience subsumes many of the countertrends in modern society, such as the attraction and even necessity of dissolution. From an unflinching look at corruption in the self and society, Lawrence's art rises, phoenixlike, to that "re-educated" or reborn vitality. For Lawrence's art is even more capacious than Leavis claimed. *Women in Love* contains the contradictions of the modern condition under an artistic control that recalls the "power" of the poet in Coleridge's definition: "This power . . . reveals itself in the balance or reconciliation of opposite or discordant qualities . . . a more than usual state of emotion, with more than usual order; judgement ever awake and steady self-possession, with enthusiasm and feeling profound or vehement."[6] As one critic has remarked, "Lawrence is the most Dostoevskian of English novelists, in whose best work conflicting ideological positions are brought into play and set against each other in a dialogue that is never simply or finally resolved."[7] In *Women in Love* Lawrence can give free play to many of these opposite and discordant qualities because he can draw on the presence-in-absence of the novel's firstborn twin, *The Rainbow.* Moreover, like Conrad and Joyce in the novel or T. S. Eliot and Ezra Pound in poetry, Lawrence widened the cultural horizon of English fiction. In its range of characters and cultural reference, *Women in Love* is a truly international novel.

The circumstances of the novel's composition suggest a last comparison, this time to the poetry of W. B. Yeats. In "Lapis Lazuli" Yeats defends the vocation of poet against certain "hysterical women," who would have him abandon the useless "gaiety" of writing to do something socially useful in time of war. Both Lawrence's novels encountered the same prejudice. In reply Yeats praises the artist's imagination, which rises above the human condition so as to survey and transfigure it. For artists, Yeats says,

> If worthy their prominent part in the play,
> Do not break up their lines to weep.

11

> They know that Hamlet and Lear are gay;
> Gaiety transfiguring all that dread . . .
> All things fall and are built again,
> And those that build them again are gay.[8]

In the closing moments of *Women in Love,* distraught at the death of Gerald, Birkin comforts himself with the thought that "the timeless creative mystery"—like the "gay" imagination in Yeats—cannot be defeated: "To be man was as nothing compared to the possibilities of the creative mystery" (580). The twin novels memorialize a world that has vanished, but they do so without nostalgia or self-pity. Elegiac pastoral coexists with utopian hopefulness. Lawrence never lost sight of either the impermanence of modern life or the inextinguishable impulse to rebuild community so as to be reborn in this life.

3

Critical Reception

Lawrence's reputation seems securely controversial, unsettling to common reader and academic specialist. Fortunately, Lawrence is in no danger of canonization. When a copy of the first edition of *Women in Love* reached Sicily from the United States, Lawrence judged it "my best book" but quickly added "It needs a bit of getting used to." The outrage of contemporary reviewers, defending themselves from the new by screaming "obscene" or "ill written," has been voiced repeatedly in the seventy years since the novel was privately published so as to escape the censors. So challenging are his vision and artistry that criticism seldom remains purely aesthetic but, willy-nilly, includes moral evaluation.

Contemporary journalists, with few exceptions, decried the "orgie of sexiness" and the view of life that "creeps and crawls" in *The Rainbow* and *Women in Love*.[1] Their reactions were, so to speak, elevated by men of letters. John Middleton Murry, who had briefly shared a house in Cornwall with the Lawrences during the writing of *Women in Love*, thought the conversations between Gerald and Birkin about *Blutbrüderschaft* had been modeled on his with Lawrence. This did not prevent him from defaming the vision of *Women in Love* as "sub-human and bestial."[2] In the first decades after publication, Lawrence was commonly charged with debasing human nature by ignoring what one obituary called the "spiritual potentialities of love as self-sacrifice or human devotion."[3] To T. S. Eliot, echoing Murry, it was obvious that Lawrence's characters not only "lose all the amenities, refinements and graces which . . . make love-making tolerable" but also "reascend the metamorphosis of evolution, passing backward beyond ape and fish to some hideous coition of protoplasm."[4] Eliot's vehement judgment inadvertently pays tribute to the originality of Lawrence's vision. Its incoherence ("reascend"?) shows the shattering effect of Lawrence on the repressive notion that lovemaking must somehow be made "tolerable."

Lawrence's alleged offenses against reticence and human nature were aggravated by his timing. The novels were published during or immediately after the world war, when patriotism could be invoked to justify the suppression of unflattering portraits of British manhood and womanhood. According to one reviewer, "A thing like *The Rainbow* has no right to exist in the wind of war."[5] In fact the judgment that *Women in Love* contained "expressions of antipathy to England" held up British publication for years.[6] Nor is the charge unfounded. In *The Rainbow* Ursula dismisses Skrebensky's argument that he "belong[s] to the nation and must do my duty by the nation" such as fighting a colonial war against the Boers in South Africa or ruling India. In *Women in Love* Birkin considers nationalism to be a form of commercialism not worth defending.

Lawrence anticipated most of this controversy. His inspiration in the English novel, Thomas Hardy, had suffered the calumny of the press for writing candidly in *Jude the Obscure* about "a deadly war waged between flesh and spirit." As Hardy wryly remarked in a postscript to *Jude*, a bishop had burned his copy of the book "probably in his despair at not being able to burn me."[7] Lawrence knew that his twin novels were "very different from *Sons and Lovers*" and its realistic forebears, "written in another language almost"; that he would need to create an audience for his innovative fiction; and that contemporary novelists, such as Arnold Bennett and John Galsworthy, would find fault.[8] Lawrence's reply to Arnold Bennett's denigration of *The Rainbow* has proved accurate: "Tell Arnold Bennett that all rules of construction hold good only for novels which are copies of other novels. A book which is not a copy of other books has its own construction, and what he calls faults, he being an old imitator, I call characteristics."[9] The history of the novel's critical reception may be summarized as the transformation of alleged "faults" into admired "characteristics."

The early reviewers disapproved of Lawrence's stylistic innovations. To John Galsworthy, the "perfervid futuristic style" was revolting and its "reiterations" boring.[10] A close friend and biographer, Catherine Carswell, who lost her job at the *Glasgow Herald* for a favorable review of *The Rainbow,* thought the more emotional passages had a "curiously vicious rhythm."[11] While conceding Lawrence's genius in descriptions of the natural world, most reviewers found fault with his language for human sexuality. Though J. M. Murry recognized that Lawrence had invented a language to reflect a new "perception" of character, he ridiculed such artistic presumption, claiming that the eyes of an ordinary reader cannot see the distinction between characters or even genders in the novel.[12]

Nowadays, Lawrence's experiments with expressive or futuristic linguistic techniques that have analogies to modern painting, his repetitions of phrase and scene that imitate the rhythms of passional experience, and his language of touch that subverts visual clichés—all seem less "faults" than "characteristics." F. R. Leavis praised the "Shakespearian" poetic and dramatic means in a chapter like "Water-Party."[13] Colin Clarke established the Romantic heritage of Lawrence's ambiguous imagery of corruption or (in Birkin's phrase) "destructive creation" and its relationship to creative renewal. Michael Ragussis has carried on Clarke's project with a linguistic study of the "new vocabulary" in *Women in Love,* in which he argues that central terms such as love and death and marriage are defined contextually but never finally. This study will contribute to an appreciation of the paradoxical language of touch. The old charges that Lawrence, unlike Joyce, was an expressive writer who paid too little attention to craft and who does not have anything interesting to say about language as a medium are no longer credible. In fact, *Women in Love* not only controls an enormous variety of language but also thematizes the relationship of words to social and psychic reality. Lawrence was well aware of the inadequacy of language either to mirror external reality or to express the life of the body. In the midst of a rumination on "love," for example, Birkin admits to the skeptical Ursula that "there was always confusion in speech . . . to know, to give utterance, was to break a way through the walls of the prison" (254).

Murry also saw accurately that Lawrence intended "to take [his readers] through this process [i.e., the African Way]."[14] Though Murry did not deny the "power of going back and re-living the vital process of pre-European civilization," he remained blind to the utopian countermovements and so judged the stylistic attempt repulsive on moral rather than aesthetic grounds. More recent criticism has demonstrated how the style allows readers to participate in both the death and rebirth of consciousness, both the dissolution of the African and European "ways" and the regeneration of "the way of freedom." Colin Clarke has defined a rhetoric of corruption in the novel; Mark Kinkead-Weekes has analyzed the process in "Moony"; and I have studied the ways Lawrence rewrote scenes in *The Rainbow* to imitate the dissolution of ordinary, repressive consciousness.

Lawrence's innovations in construction in *Women in Love* went unappreciated by early reviewers who preferred the norm of the bildungsroman, with its affinity to biography and historical narrative. When one reviewer noted the analogy to "ritual," she leapt to the conclusion that Lawrence was less a novelist than a "priest of an age": "he consciously desires what all ritual infers, the release of individuality in the confusion of sense."[15] As a keen student of anthropology, Lawrence did indeed adapt ritual elements from drama in an attempt to "release" a cramped individuality; however, the sexual consequences are not a confusion but a renewal. The abrupt, disjunctive progress of the plot in *Women in Love,* which contributed to the success of its adaptation to the screen, remains underrated. Herbert Read mocked Angus Wilson's comparison of the novel's form to "a court dance." More recently, J. Hillis Miller has written about repetition in Victorian and modern novels without once mentioning *The Rainbow* or *Women in Love,* though the twin novels are as subtle performances of structural and linguistic repetition as any by those authors whom Miller singles out: Emily Brontë, Thackeray, Hardy, Conrad, and Woolf.[16]

In the representation of human nature Lawrence's intentions were radical. As he explained to his first editor, Edward Garnett, who wanted him to continue mining the realistic vein of *Sons and Lovers:* "that which is physic—non-human, in humanity, is more interesting to me than the old-fashioned human element."[17] A decade later, though admiring *A Passage to India,* he wrote: "Life is more interesting in its undercurrents than in its obvious; and E. M. [Forster] does see people, people, and nothing but people: *ad nauseam.*"[18] Forster, in turn, thought Lawrence "the greatest imaginative novelist of his time" but doubted the truth of his characters: "The quaint quartet in *Women in Love*—have you ever met young men and women like that?"[19] The novelist who had been lauded for character portrayal in *Sons and Lovers* was now accused of depicting "strange avatars" and "animals on the prowl" but certainly not moral or spiritual beings. A reviewer of *The Rainbow* fumed: "If men and women are just this and nothing more, then the imaginative literature of the world is false from Homer down."[20] To her notebook Katherine Mansfield confided the horrified feeling that "Lawrence had possessed an animal and fallen under a curse."[21] Together Murry and Mansfield accurately judged that Lawrence had become "the outlaw of modern English literature."[22] From the wild horses in *The Rainbow* through horse, cat, and rabbit in *Women in Love* to the fox, bear, cow, reptile, and fish of later animal fables and poems, Lawrence insists on the identity between human and animal. Gods from Homer, Greek tragedy, the Bible, and so-called primitive societies permeate his fiction as expressions of this dual vision or mythic realism. The mythological Lawrence has found favor in the

United States in contrast to the emphasis in England on the social historian in F. R. Leavis's great tradition of George Eliot, Henry James, and Joseph Conrad. American critics such as J. B. Vickery, W. Y. Tindall, and James Cowan have concentrated on later, less realistic works like *The Plumed Serpent, Lady Chatterley's Lover,* and *The Escaped Cock.* This study explores the blending of the two Lawrences, the realist and the mythologist.

Similarly, when John Galsworthy or T. S. Eliot charged that Lawrence makes sex the central mystery of human life at the expense of a disembodied "soul," they were accurate but beside the point. For Lawrence the definition of sex is as broad as married love: "And what is sex, after all, but the symbol of the relation of man to woman, woman to man? And the relation of man to woman is wide as all life. It consists in infinite different flows between the two beings, different, even apparently contrary. Chastity is part of the flow between man and woman, as is physical passion."[23] *The Rainbow* presents a prothalamion or marriage song across two generations, and in the third generation Ursula finally achieves an epithalamion or nuptial song with Birkin in "Excurse."

Another irony in Lawrence's reputation centers on his depiction of the Brangwen sisters' quest for a place in a largely man's world. One early reviewer focused her objections to Lawrence's irrationalism on his images of women: "There is all the difference in the world between Shakespeare's attitude towards Lear or Lady Macbeth and this author's attitude towards Anna dancing to God or Ursula in her vampire mood."[24] What the reviewer considers a weakness, however, is actually a strength. Ursula and Gudrun challenge and defeat a repressive patriarchy. These heroines act not only with the spirit of Lady Macbeth, but even more with that of the heroines in Shakespeare's comedies, such as Rosalind in *As You Like It* or Olivia in *Twelfth Night,* and perhaps most of all with that of the formidable women in Greek tragedy—Agave, Medea, and Clytemnestra, who take terrible vengeance on the men who have betrayed them. Too often it is forgotten that Ursula Brangwen, as created in both novels, is one of the most fully rounded heroines in all of world literature.

Just as Lawrence "re-sourced" the novel by making it "more the joint work of man and woman," he was ahead of his time in re-creating the love between men not only in itself but as a complement to heterosexual marriage. For this achievement he has never received his critical due. His English publisher, worried about the frank portrayal of homoerotic affection, muted several passages. An early reviewer judged the wrestling scene in "Gladiatorial" to be "sheer filth" and likely to deprave young boys.[25] Then, in *Son of Woman,* John Middleton Murry advanced the theory that Lawrence's oedipal complex, as re-created in *Sons and Lovers,* had prevented him from loving a woman and that, in recoil from that failure, he sought the love of a man. According to Murry, the art directly reflected Lawrence's life and explained the failure of Birkin with both Ursula and Gerald. T. S. Eliot endorsed this reductive theory in a review of Murry entitled "The Victim and the Sacrificial Knife."[26] Many commentators have followed Murry's lead by confusing art with life, thereby distorting both. According to one biographer, for example, "the publication of the suppressed Prologue [in 1963] . . . made all previous biographical writing out of date."[27] This study offers an aesthetic rationale for the homoerotic theme, based on the evidence of Lawrence's intentions in the heavily rewritten manuscripts.

Lawrence's manuscripts have transformed the way we view his craft. Many early reviewers and critics, amazed by his prolific output, justified their objections to Lawrence's stylistic experiments by declaring him careless, too eagerly proselytizing to master his craft. Champions like Aldous Huxley revalued this image by invoking a Romantic "daimon" to which the writer gave "another chance to say what it had to say."[28] But scholars have since found that what Leavis called "the immense labour of art" in *The Rainbow* and *Women in Love* included not only multiple drafts but the control of vast structures. Local revisions inspired others across fictional generations and counterpointed chapters, as manuscript studies by Mark Kinkead-Weekes, Charles Ross, and Keith Sagar have shown. Lawrence the craftsman evolved fictional means to control his penchant for prophecy. As he remarked apropos a criticism of Thomas Hardy, "if I don't 'subdue my art to a metaphysic' . . . I do write because I want folk—English folk—to alter, and have more sense."[29] There was more than a little of the Salvator Mundi in Lawrence as well as in Birkin. Treatises and reviews, filled with advice on how people could live better, poured from his pen. But he turned this creative habit to fictional advantage as a theme in the novels. All the characters debate the modern crisis and challenge each other's theories. H. M. Daleski's *The Forked Flame* and Frank Kermode's *Lawrence* led the way in exploring how "the visionary is contained by the novelist."[30] By now, however, their methodological example has hardened into an allegorizing of the work that may obscure the crucial distinction between a fictional character and the writer in real life or in works of nonfiction. Though Lawrence was a philosophical novelist as well as a social historian and mythic realist, he did not erect a "system" as did William Blake or W. B. Yeats; nor did he write to test ideas, as it has become fashionable to claim. Lawrence's motto was: "Art-speech is the only truth. An artist is usually a damned liar, but his art, if it be art, will tell you the truth of his day. . . . Never trust the artist. Trust the tale."[31] And we shall.

The *Rainbow* and *Women in Love* have gained a secure place in that modern pantheon of taste, the university curriculum. But Lawrence still makes the guardians of culture uneasy. One academic critic, for example, has recently pigeonholed *Women in Love* as "perhaps the most unpleasant important novel in the language."[32] With advocates like that, Lawrence needs no detractors. At this moment of equivocal praise, therefore, a fresh reading of the novel seems called for.

A Reading

4

"Prologue": An Abandoned Beginning

The fragmentary first draft of *Women in Love* provides a fascinating glimpse of Lawrence at work. The two surviving chapters, "Prologue" and "The Wedding," differ strikingly from the published novel in their treatment both of the affair between Hermione Roddice and Rupert Birkin and of the friendship between Birkin and Gerald Crich. The fragment also lacks salient features of the published novel: the opening conversation of Ursula and Gudrun; any hint of an attraction between Gerald Crich and Gudrun Brangwen, much less the "strange transport" Gudrun feels at first sight of Gerald; any suggestion that Gerald is an industrial magnate or that his physiognomy has symbolic resonance; and any sign that Lawrence's authorial voice will be distinguished from that of his fictional likeness, Rupert Birkin.

As the chapter opens Birkin and Gerald are sharing a skiing holiday four years before the marriage day of Laura Crich, the day on which the published novel begins. Although drawn into a "trembling nearness," the two men retain a "complete reserve," concealing their unspoken love. A week of mountain sports passes like an intense brief lifetime, and the friends part with the "submerged" knowledge that "they loved each other, that each would die for the other." Birkin returns to his post as inspector of schools and his hopeless affair with Hermione Roddice, who has "worshiped" him for the five years since he was a fellow of Magdalen College writing brilliant essays on education.

The emotional and sexual impasse reached by Birkin and Hermione recalls the worst moments between Paul Morel and Miriam Leivers in *Sons and Lovers* or between Jude Fawley and Sue Bridehead in *Jude the Obscure*, a favorite novel that Lawrence had scrutinized in *Study of Thomas Hardy* less than two years before. Birkin, like Paul and Jude, develops a "monomania" for physical fulfillment, while Hermione, like Miriam and Sue, can offer only spiritual intimacy or resign herself to a willed sensual response. But in "Prologue," unlike the novels, the responsibility for failure clearly rests with the man, Birkin, who vacillates between Hermione's "sacrificial" sexuality and even more degraded sex with "slightly bestial prostitutes" that leaves him ever "more hollow." The reason is that he denies his attraction to men, first revealed in his love for Gerald Crich:

> All the time, he recognized that, although he was always drawn to women, feeling more at home with a woman than with a man, yet it was for men that he felt the hot, flushing, roused attraction which a man is supposed to feel for the other sex. Although nearly all his living interchange went on with one woman or another, although he was terribly intimate with at least one woman, and practically never intimate with a man, yet the male physique had a fascination for him, and for the female physique he felt only a fondness, a sort of sacred love, as for a sister.[1]

But Birkin, whose physical description resembles Lawrence's, will not admit the "*beauté mâle*," despising his innate feelings yet drawn to "exchange intimacy" with men. Nor can he love the whole person of the men to whom he is attracted. Just as he is split in his relations with women between spiritual affection and lust, so he looks on the men of his secret desire as physical specimens but not intellectual companions. In fact, his feelings are shaped by a class consciousness similar to that in the homosexual literature of the late Victorian and Edwardian years.[2] Throughout the chapter Birkin is drawn to "ruddy, well-nourished fellows, good-natured and easy"—that is, men who are intellectually if not socially inferior but physically desirable. Birkin enjoys having Gerald, a "hard-limbed traveler and sportsman," in his power: "Birkin felt a passion of desire for Gerald Crich, for the clumsier, cruder intelligence and the limited soul, and for the striving, unlightened body of his friend." Gerald reciprocates with a "reverence" for the higher understanding of the physically frail Birkin whom he can protect with his superior physical strength. But Birkin suppresses these homosexual desires, avoiding any "demonstration" of affection that might recall the passionate friendship of David and Jonathan in the Old Testament.

This incapacity either to love women or to admit love for men, which seems an inevitable symptom of the degeneracy of the times, provokes despair and fatalism: "And Birkin was just coming to a knowledge of the essential futility of all attempts at social unanimity in constructiveness. In the winter, there can only be unanimity of disintegration. . . . He ran about from death to death. Work was terrible, horrible because he did not believe in it. . . . In his private life the same horror of futility and wrongness dogged him."[3] Since the voices of Birkin and Lawrence seem identical in "Prologue," such despair is never questioned or qualified. Indeed, authorial defensiveness continues through the next, penultimate version of *Women in Love,* preventing Lawrence from imagining *Blutbrüderschaft* as a regenerative relationship in a world of death.

The fragmentary second chapter of this draft, "The Wedding," also differs strikingly from "Sisters" of the published novel. Here the authorial manner is clumsily sociological, telling rather than showing the reader that the sisters have "that look of blighted expectation which disfigures the young, eager women who have settled down to earning their own living."[4] Ursula's detestation of the home is decided and conscious, like Birkin's knowledge of his homosexual inclinations in "Prologue." This finality of judgment would have left little room for development. In the published novel, as we shall see, Ursula is initially shocked by Gudrun's antagonism to home life and apologetic for the sordidness of the countryside. All in all, one cannot easily imagine where the novel would have gone after this pessimistic opening. Nor, evidently, could Lawrence. He abandoned the draft with only a few chapters completed.

5

"Sisters": Beginning as Ending

To begin is always uncertain, next door to chaos. To begin requires
that, uncertainly, we bid farewell to some thing, some one, some
where, some time. Beginning is still ending.

—Angus Fletcher[1]

It would be an exaggeration to claim that all of *Women in Love* is
prefigured in its first chapter, "Sisters," as Hugh Kenner claims that
the first two pages of James Joyce's *A Portrait of the Artist as a Young
Man* "enact the entire action in microcosm."[2] Nonetheless, the opening
of *Women in Love* is every bit as contrapuntal as *Portrait*, and the
musical analogy points to what a reader of John Keats's "Ode on a
Grecian Urn" might call the "unheard" melodies of *The Rainbow* that
Lawrence plays throughout its sequel, *Women in Love*.

The novel opens deceptively with a domestic scene of two sisters
chatting about marriage, customarily the principle topic of unmarried
women. They are embroidering and painting, those typical pursuits
of cultivated young women in Victorian society and fiction. Having
experimented in "Prologue" with an opening that focused on men,
Lawrence now gave the fictional initiative to those "self-responsible"

27

Brangwen sisters. To the sisters, marriage seems both the "inevitable next step" and "impossible," made so by "the man." If the man seems unappealing, perhaps children would be an incentive? No, that too proves an unconvincing argument. Children arouse in Gudrun "no feeling at all" and in Ursula only one of incapacity ("it is still beyond one"). The wit of these liberated women at the expense of the male sex and conventional wisdom about the role of woman, however, is qualified by an undertow of "bitterness" and "fright" at the blank prospect before a woman who chooses not to marry. Their conversation uncovers a "void" caused by lack of faith in conventional marriage as a means of continuity. Are this fear and confusion about the future actually the price of their freedom? From the perspective of Lawrence's Brangwensaga, the sisters' conversation implies a radical discontinuity, from whose "edge" they draw back. But the question hangs in the air. As Gudrun admits uneasily, she has returned home from the life of a free woman in the world of bohemian artists to find an eligible man. Ursula too is chagrined by her status as an unwed schoolmistress living at home. If we know Ursula's history from *The Rainbow,* her anguished feelings of unfulfillment, here and later, appear more plausible.

At the end of *Sons and Lovers,* Paul Morel had to bridge the gap between, on the one hand, a "baptism of fire in passion" with Clara that might arrest the personal "drift toward death" and, on the other, the man's world of public history.[3] In the pastoral opening of *The Rainbow,* the tragically unreconciled impulses of *Sons and Lovers* are universalized in the anonymous Brangwens and located in the arena of marriage. The mythic vantage of the opening section allows Lawrence to pose the largest questions about man's destiny: How do men and women express the universal rhythms of nature in modern society without disinheriting themselves? Can men and women preserve the plenitude of the Brangwen men's response to nature ("the source of generation") while venturing into the "unknown" of history, to which the Brangwen women aspire? In retrospect the visionary opening is also a source of irony. The modern world into which Ursula ventures for freedom and self-expression turns out to be less a "beyond" than an end, hostile to her. Then marriage in *Women in Love* seems to be either impossible for the free-spirited Brangwen sisters or a form of wedlock for the young man in "A Chair" who is marrying a young woman he has made pregnant. The latter couple recalls another in Thomas Hardy's *Jude the Obscure* whose appearance at the registry office is so repellant that Jude Fawley and Sue Bridehead, waiting their turn, postpone marriage indefinitely. Has marriage been reduced to a social or biological trap?

To read some influential feminist criticism, one might well think so. According to Carolyn Heilbrun, for example, "the most lasting novels" of modern literature depict marriage as "the most sinister of arrangements . . . a process of victimization."[4] Her examples are James Joyce's *Dubliners,* Ford Madox Ford's *The Good Soldier,* and *The Rainbow*. Rather than finding Lawrence a gratifying exception to her rule, Heilbrun travesties and dismisses the accomplishment of an artist who dared to imagine the full flowering of human life in marriage: "Lawrence's *The Rainbow* could qualify as a disquisition upon the failure of marriage. From this failure there emerges an individual, Ursula. But [in] *Women in Love,* Lawrence can see her only as the mate for the proper man; married to him, she disappears from the novel. Lawrence tells us that the marriage succeeded, but even so he does not lie to us. He allows us to see that Ursula is an appendage, and little more."[5] This distorts, as we shall see, everything in the novel—artistic intention, plot, and thematic development. Because it is representative, Heilbrun's misreading requires a closer look.

Heilbrun asserts that marriage in modern English fiction appears as "a failed institution in which passion is not supported by friendship." It is not clear whether artists have reflected the modern condition or refused to imagine more adequate relationships or both. The implied normative values are the watchwords of feminism, such as "mutuality" or "mutual respect between equals" or "a room of one's own"—all incontestably desirable. When applied to fiction, however, these norms result in judgments that place greater value on friendship than on passion. Thus, Thomas Hardy's *Far from the Madding Crowd* is an "important marriage novel" because, in arranging for Bathsheba to accept loyal Gabriel Oak after the deaths of the young, passionate Sergeant Troy and older, obsessive Farmer Boldwood, Hardy "emphasized the possibility of friendship and mutuality, rather than the glamour of romance."[6] A reader who empathizes with Bathsheba's spirit will more likely agree with Lawrence that, though Gabriel will be a good husband, "the flower of imaginative first love is dead for [Bathsheba] with Troy's scorn of her."[7] Similarly, in Virginia Woolf's *Mrs. Dalloway,* Clarissa's decision to reject the romantically importunate Peter Walsh for the proper, passionless Richard Dalloway seems to Heilbrun "correct" on the grounds that Peter would have forced them always "unnaturally together" whereas Richard leaves Clarissa largely to herself. Heilbrun concedes that the marriage is "not ideal, in any romantic sense" but urges that the freedom Clarissa possesses to remain Clarissa within her role as Mrs. Dalloway is more valuable than passion: "Surely this, rather than development toward a greater dependence, is the proper movement within a marriage."[8] In short, Heilbrun assumes that passion and friendship hardly ever coexist in a marriage and that, given the choice, a woman should prefer companionship. This is cold comfort in art as in life. What Heilbrun refuses to admit is that marriage with both passion and friendship has been depicted in English fiction by, among others, D. H. Lawrence. Other critics may defend the liveliness, erotic and friendly, in marriage as imagined by James Joyce—to do which, of course, they would turn to Leopold and Molly Bloom in *Ulysses.* My task is to demonstrate that Brangwen women never condescend to be mere "appendages" of men.

One brief scene between father and suitor, those pillars of patriarchal power, will suggest the strength and independence of women in Lawrence that Heilbrun undervalues. In "Moony" Birkin arrives unexpectedly to propose to Ursula and, finding her out, explains his call to her father. Throughout the novel Birkin sharply criticizes conventional marriage and common notions of "love," often to the amusement of Ursula, who remains healthily skeptical of both ordinary marriage and Birkin's utopian plans. On the previous evening they debate love and "service," with Ursula accusing Birkin of being "egocentric" and Birkin replying hotly, "I wouldn't give a straw for your female ego—it's a rag doll" (326–27). Though avowing love for her, he resists the temptation of "the old destructive fires" of sexuality and so Ursula leaves wistfully. The next morning Birkin recognizes his willfulness—"perhaps he had been wrong to go to her with an idea of what he wanted"—and sets out impulsively to propose. But the conversation with her father goes badly. Birkin annoys Will Brangwen by saying that "If one repents being married, the marriage is at an end" and that he's sure Ursula will "please herself." The father angrily retorts:

> "I would rather bury them, than see them getting into a lot of loose ways such as you see everywhere nowadays.—I'd rather bury them—"
> "Yes, but, you see," said Birkin . . . "they won't give either you or me the chance to bury them, because they're not to be buried." (336)

Nor will Brangwen women be bullied, as we learn when Ursula returns, finds the two men glowering at her, and coolly refuses to give Birkin any answer at all to his proposal: "You do this off your *own* bat, it has nothing to do with me" (339). Ursula neither disappears from the novel nor becomes an appendage of Birkin.

6

"Remarkable Females":
Lawrence and Women

Having read the very first attempt at "The Sisters," Edward Garnett commented dryly on its "remarkable females." Nothing survives of this draft, but the predicament of extraordinary women facing imprisonment in ordinary life lay close to Lawrence's heart throughout his career. Louisa Lindley in "Daughters of the Vicar" (1914) watches her sister Mary bow to family pressure, marry a man who "lacked the full range of human feelings," and, in so doing, "murder" her body.[1] Louisa rebels and, despite the class-motivated disapproval of her family, follows a true fate in marrying a miner's son and emigrating. In "The Horse-Dealer's Daughter" (1921), Mabel Pervin, who has sacrificed her youth serving a motherless family of rough but financially respectable men, faces becoming a "skivvy" after the collapse of the horse business. She is rescued from a suicide attempt and then forces her rescuer, a repressed country doctor, to admit his love for her. In *The Lost Girl* (1920) Alvina Houghton, who is Ursula's age, faces a bleak future as a spinster attendant on her father. Convinced that modern women feel the humiliation of failure more keenly than men, the narrator of the novel concocts "extraordinary" means to rescue its heroine from the "ordinary fate" in life and fiction of employment or "marriage with some dull school-teacher or office-clerk."[2] As the title implies, only by "losing" herself in conventional terms can Alvina succeed in life. She joins a touring theatrical troupe and falls in love with an Italian, but their love seems impossible in its provincial setting. Then Alvina must decide whether to accept a proposal from a prominent, middle-aged doctor. As a qualified midwife she does not need to marry the doctor, but by doing so she would avoid the slings and arrows of social discomfort. At the crisis, it is as much her possession of a "magic potentiality" in her own femaleness as the sensual spell of her Italian lover Ciccio that compels her to reject the rewards of class and social revenge.[3] To Miss Pinnegar's horrified "You're a lost girl," she defiantly replies, "I like being lost." And as she sails for Italy, she associates the "ash-grey coffin" of England sinking on the horizon with home. The plot of *The Lost Girl* prefigures Connie Chatterley's notorious escape from Wragby Hall in *Lady Chatterley's Lover* (1928).

Finally, in the posthumously published novella *The Virgin and the Gipsy* (1930), Yvette must escape the oppressive rectory where family life is dominated by a manipulative grandmother, "the Mater," and her son, the rector, whose emotional dishonesty has already driven Yvette's mother to desert the family. To Yvette home means the condition of feeling "deflowered" and "defiled." The story teaches her to have more courage in her body. Though rescue comes through the mysterious Gipsy, her inner strength would have devised some means of escape. In sum, these extraordinary women achieve liberation and actual or potential fulfillment by their own initiatives, though often with the aid of men.

Lawrence's heroines are self-begetters who sever family bonds in the interest of personal renewal, thereby both emulating and deviating from their orphaned predecessors in the nineteenth-century novel— for example, Emma Woodhouse, Jane Eyre, Esther Summerson, Tess Durbeyfield. In her dispiriting position as unwed teacher living at home or in her judgment that Birkin is a "prig," Ursula may recall Elizabeth Bennett in *Pride and Prejudice,* who is in "want" of a husband and liable to misjudge the reserved Darcy. Both Elizabeth and Ursula bring wit and self-mockery to relationships with men who are too impressed with themselves. Ursula's idealism, injured but undaunted at the start of *Women in Love,* also bears some resemblance to that of Dorothea Brooke in *Middlemarch.* Ursula has always yearned for one of the "sons of God" and been disappointed by unworthy incarnations as well as the failure of the world to conform to her visions. "She had the ash of disillusion gritting under her teeth. . . . Always the shining doorway was a gate into another ugly yard, dirty and active and dead," as she reflects in *The Rainbow.*[4]

One reason Ursula cherishes the ideal of the sons of God from Genesis is that she wants a lover without background, one with whom she can shape an unprecedented destiny. This would have been a solution to Tess Durbeyfield's predicament with the family name in *Tess of the D'Urbervilles,* where genealogy is an inescapable trap. Hence, amid all Lawrence's sympathy for Tess, who is caught between the caddishly physical Alec and the perversely spiritual Angel, one detects in his *Study of Thomas Hardy* an impatience at her acceptance of responsibility for the seduction and its aftermath in Angel Clare's revulsion. Angel Clare, who falls in love with a vision of Tess's "rustic innocence," cannot maintain a sense of her identity after she confesses her seduction by Alec D'Urberville: "O Tess, forgiveness does not apply to the case! You were one person; now you are another."[5] Tess pleads that she remains "my very self" despite defilement, but Angel believes she has become "another woman in your shape." Yearning to rewrite the novel, Lawrence chides Tess for not forcing Angel to recognize his error and to accept the female principle of life. In Lawrence, as in Jane Austen or George Eliot or Thomas Hardy, the state of being single or virgin or celibate—which Lawrence prefers to call "chaste"— is never considered an absence or defect but a potentiality. The indomitable women of Greek tragedy, such as Agave, Antigone, Medea, or Phaedra, inspired him for similar reasons.[6] Their spirit is rekindled in the Brangwen sisters, whose story can be called a revisionary continuation of many female histories in the nineteenth-century novel.

Lawrence's defense of women extends to criticism of another

literary precursor, Leo Tolstoy, for "giving in" to public opinion and treating Anna's adultery with Vronsky in *Anna Karenina* as a sin rather than "a consummation devoutly to be wished."[7] As a critic Lawrence rewrote novels not only to protect strong heroines from their authors but to prepare for a continuing engagement with "the germ" of his Brangwensaga: "woman becoming individual, self-responsible, taking her own initiative." Lawrence exalts what Ursula calls the "gorgeous female self" in challenge to a patriarchal society.

In the opening chapter of *Women in Love,* we notice the "look of sensitive expectancy" on Ursula's face. The word *expectancy* carries the meaning of pregnancy and childbirth, which is a characteristic metaphor for personal and generational growth in *The Rainbow*. But what is there for the Brangwen sisters to be expectant about? If not marriage, what does the future hold? They have escaped from an unsettling conversation about marriage by going out to view a wedding and one for which "Ursula felt almost responsible. . . . [It] must not be a fiasco" (65). Her feelings seem less strange if we know that in *The Rainbow* she breaks a long engagement with Anton Skrebensky and then suffers a miscarriage. In any case, the only participant besides the bridal couple who seems to enjoy the wedding is Will Brangwen, the father of the skeptical sisters: "He would enjoy playing a wedding march" (69). Considering that the sisters find their parents' home stifling and have just mocked marriage, the tone of their remark must be ironic.

That this escape from thought will be brief, moreover, seems a condition of the sisters' social life. Images of entrapment or imprisonment abound in the chapter and throughout the novel. Gudrun "clung" to Ursula for support amid the alien population of home, giving Ursula a feeling of "constraint" and a desire to be "alone, freed from the enclosure" of her sister's personality. Hermione, who is unable to "escape" from thoughts of insufficiency, desperately hopes a permanent "conjunction" with Birkin will somehow "close up this deficiency." That is a reason for marriage that the Brangwen sisters have already rejected. Later, marriage undertaken for that reason leads to disaster, as when Gerald turns to Gudrun to fill the "void" exposed by the death of his father and his own flagging interest in public life. Finally, Gudrun and Birkin feel "possessed" by Gerald and Hermione. For Birkin it is ominously the possession of "fate"—a word already used to describe the trap of marriage.

In sum, Ursula's witty skepticism about marriage but suppressed affection for children; her look of expectancy and "strange prescience" recalling the characteristic Brangwen "look of an inheritor"; and the analogy to childbirth that she uses to suggest her predicament ("if only she could break through the last integuments")—all these show her to be a Brangwen. In their opening dialogue, the sisters have restated and revalued the generational concerns of *The Rainbow*. Home is where you escape from, marriage is what you avoid as "impossible," and childbirth is what seems "beyond one."

Genealogy of the Brangwen Family

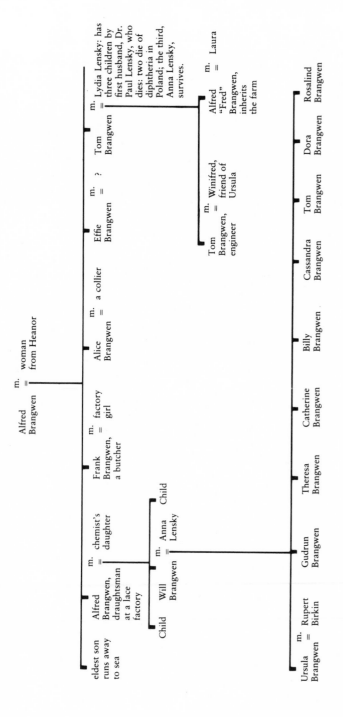

7

Marriage

This then was marriage! . . . All that mattered was that he should love her and she should love him and they should live kindled to one another, like the Lord in two burning bushes that were not consumed.

—Will Brangwen in "Anna Victrix," *The Rainbow*

'Slike when you're dead—you're a long time married.

—pregnant bride-to-be in "A Chair," *Women in Love*

Human continuity and marriage are intertwined. So the opening revaluation of all generational concepts—home, marriage, children—raises questions about both the relationship of the Brangwens to history, past and present, and the relationship of the novel to its precursor or twin in the Brangwensaga. In what sense is *Women in Love*, as Lawrence claimed, a "sequel" to *The Rainbow*? We may approach an answer by way of genealogy.

Both rootedness and transcendence mark the Brangwens. In *The Rainbow* the English Brangwens of the first two generations (ca. 1840–90) are enriched by foreign admixture—the marriage of Tom Brangwen to the Polish widow, Lydia Lensky—and intermarriage between Anna Lensky Brangwen and her cousin, Will Brangwen. Then, in the third generation (ca. 1880–1905), Ursula's first love is Anton Skrebensky, descendent of her grandmother's friend and fellow exile, Baron Skrebensky. Just as individual Brangwens are rooted in England yet expectant of the beyond, or fixed in local history yet ever seeking transcendence as imagined in the motif of a quest for the promised land, so too the family evolves in a pattern of change within continuity.

The first Brangwens, who live at the Marsh farm, are "a curious family, a law to themselves, separate from the world, isolated, a small republic set in invisible bounds."[1] Anna, Ursula's mother, defies her parents by marrying her cousin at the age of eighteen, cruelly reminding Tom Brangwen, her stepfather, "*You* are not my father—my father is dead";[2] yet she lives nearby in Cossethay and brings her marital problems to the Marsh, confiding in Tom that she is pregnant before she tells her husband. Will and Anna are the transitional generation of the Brangwens, settled like their parents in the Marsh world but unsatisfied with a life of self-absorption and more troubled by their relation to society. Anna becomes "Victrix" by finding a purpose for her life in childbearing and by fighting off Will's claims to masculine supremacy in the household. Will cannot exercise his father's patriarchal power but shows through his interest in painting, carving, and architectural history a widening cultural horizon as well as a growing frustration with the bounds of his life. In "The Cathedral" chapter, the Brangwens are deprived of belief in religion as a spiritual, as opposed to customary, "rhythm of eternity in a ragged, inconsequential life."[3] Under the probing of skeptical Anna, Will loses his "absolute," retaining only a nostalgic affection for "the old dear form of worship."[4] When Ursula and Skrebensky visit a church a generation later, her feeling that "the place echoed desolate" recalls her father's feeling that Lincoln Cathedral has become "a shapely heap of dead matter." Will's disillusionment becomes representative in this historical perspective. Organized religion commands no belief in *Women in Love*, except as one of the "old institutions" Hermione's pompous brother Alexander, a member of Parliament, likes to "keep up."

Then at the crisis of the second generation, Will and Anna,

advancing like their parents through sexual experience, find themselves forgetting children and home and thereby forging a new, "purposive" relationship with the world outside, signaled by Will's involvement in the education movement as a handicraft instructor at the local school: "the house by the yew trees was in connection with the great human endeavour at last. It gained a new vigour thereby."[5] The paradoxical imaginative logic of this transition in "The Child" chapter, which was actually the last part of the novel Lawrence revised, has been disputed by critics.[6] But it is incontestable that for Will and Anna, unlike their parents, sex becomes primarily a means of self-expression rather than procreation. Already in the second generation of *The Rainbow*, then, progress depends less on actual inheritance. Childbearing, with its analogies to rebirth in the natural world, has become an uncertain way forward.

In the third generation, which extends into the present of *Women in Love*, the young Ursula resents her mother's fecundity, which fills the house with children. Since she is in reaction from domesticity, it is symbolically fitting that her dance with Skrebensky at a harvest wedding feast, which repeats her parents' courtship dance in a moonlit cornfield, should become a fierce contest of wills, a battle for supremacy rather than a rhythm of mutuality. The imagery of the two moon scenes is starkly different. Whereas her parents Will and Anna reconcile dark and light in the context of the season, work, and love, Ursula expresses her female identity by "annihilating" Skrebensky in an embrace of "corrosive" force under the brilliant but for him baleful light of a moon allied to female independence. Then Ursula enters "The Man's World" of schoolteaching without the support of either her family or Skrebensky, who has gone to serve his country in the Boer War. The price of her entry proves to be the "violation" of her nature in a constant battle against the children and the system of education that imprisons them both. Nor can she escape into the educated elite. The university turns out to be merely a "sham warehouse" in which knowledge is produced for commercial profit. Doubly disappointed in these public debuts, Ursula renews the affair with Skrebensky, though she knows deep in her heart that he cannot lead her into the "unknown." She hesitates to marry and become the wife of a military officer in colonial India. The crisis again occurs under the moon; again the willful woman asserts her freedom by psychologically destroying her man. The overmastered Skrebensky slinks away, hurriedly marries his captain's daughter, and sails for India. Learning belatedly that she is pregnant, Ursula writes him a contrite letter in which she promises to be an obedient wife if he will take her back. Just as the moon had symbolically forbidden her to marry Skrebensky, however, a herd of wild horses, real but also projections of her inner turmoil, so frighten her one day while she is out walking alone that she miscarries Skrebensky's child. The natural law, Lawrence seems to be saying, will not allow Ursula to subordinate her "gorgeous female self" to conventional wifehood; certainly, the miscarriage liberates her from the "compression" of Anton's world. In terms of the novel's generational theme, Ursula must miscarry the child of the lover who is identified with the status quo. This prepares her for the arrival of one of the sons of God, for whom she has been searching since adolescence. The psychological rebirth of the individual has become actually as well as metaphorically separate from natural childbirth. The typical Brangwen metaphor of death and rebirth has lost its original meaning: there seems to be no social expression in work or family for the individual's instinctual life. The arching rainbow of the final pages may promise but cannot fulfill the previous Brangwen inheritance of a rooted history and a connection with the beyond.

In *Women in Love*, personal and familial continuity in the modern world must proceed through discontinuity. The metaphor of rebirth all but disappears, having become anachronistic in a world dominated by images of generational death rather than renewal. Moreover, Ursula's experience has broken the genealogical sequence of the Brangwen-saga by making her feel originless: "I have no father nor mother nor lover . . . no allocated place in the world of . . . Beldover . . . Nottingham . . . England . . . this world"[7]—a sentiment she repeats at the end of *Women in Love*.

Marriage

This myth of history in *The Rainbow* explains the alienation of Ursula and the main characters in *Women in Love*. Deprived of faith in such mediating institutions as church, school, army, and industry, the Brangwens cannot find the means to express themselves in the modern world. Ursula's disastrous attempt to seek in sexual experience a privileged form of expression foreshadows the fate of Gerald and Gudrun, who, having become cynical of marriage as a way of uniting work and love, pursue sensual "abandon" to its tragic consequences. The characters in *Women in Love* search for a social outlet at home or abroad, tempted meanwhile to pursue sexual experience as a form of salvation. As many critics have noted disapprovingly, Ursula's vision of a world transformed for both natural aristocrats and common people beneath a symbolic rainbow in the final pages of *The Rainbow* is wishful thinking. Ursula is in the precarious position of Lawrence, who, after his travels around the world, wrote to the social psychologist Trigant Burrows: "There is no repression of the sexual individual comparable to the repression of the societal man in me."[8] But Ursula's vision of "the earth's new architecture," which may be unconvincing if interpreted as Lawrence's prophecy, is perfectly appropriate to Ursula's personal history—her Brangwenian wish, renewed in *Women in Love*, to find expression in social forms for the personal, sexual self that is also linked to nature.

8

History, Repetition, and Paternity

Pray for yourselves to God, for there's no help for you from your parents.

—Mrs. Crich in "Death and Love," *Women in Love*

Paternity and patriarchal authority as the agencies of continuity are first established and then discredited in the course of Lawrence's double novel. Lawrence began with a contemporary love story of Ella, Ben Templeman, Birkin, Gerald, Gudrun, and Loerke. Then he progressed backwards to find the generational roots of these modern couples, adding two previous generations, the parents and grandparents of Ursula and Gudrun. In the process "The Sisters" turned into a Brangwensaga. Yet the third generation of *The Rainbow* questions generational succession by reversing the metaphorical sequence of birth-death-rebirth. Ursula miscarries Skrebensky's child after the encounter with the horses, thereby symbolically casting out her thoughts of being a submissive wife. She cannot deny the "horses" within her and must await one of the sons of God.

Whatever weight we give to these countergenerational forces, however, *The Rainbow* confirms the sustaining nature of paternity.

Women in Love, on the contrary, dramatizes the reactionary, even deadly force of paternity as well as the need for natural aristocrats to divest themselves of family in order to find a new self in discontinuity rather than continuity. The novel opens with the sisters disparaging both marriage and maternity; continues with them rejecting their parents, who have been reduced to mere ciphers since *The Rainbow;* and ends as Ursula and Birkin get married without parental blessing, decide never to have a home, and finally repudiate both their old identity and the world that sustained it: "She thought of the Marsh, the old, intimate farm-life at Cossethay. My God, how far was she projected from her childhood, how far was she still to go! In one lifetime one travelled through aeons. The great chasm of memory . . . was so great, that it seemed she had no identity, that the child she had been . . . was a little creature of history, not really herself. . . . If only [Birkin] could call a world into being, that should be their own world!" (481–82).

Yet just as there was a countermovement to generational progress in *The Rainbow,* so in *Women in Love* there is a movement countering the drift toward discontinuity. As Birkin and Ursula motor to the consummation of their love in "Excurse," for example, Ursula recalls that her parents, Will and Anna, also visited Southwell during their courtship, to see the Minster and have tea at the Saracen's Head inn. Ursula's sudden memory not only returns her momentarily to "the dream-world of one's childhood," though now she has become "a strange, transcendent reality," but also sets up the recognition scene, in which Birkin appears to her as "not a man . . . something more" (394–95). She has finally found one of the sons of God for whom she has been searching since her youth in *The Rainbow.* Thus, new significance grows out of reenactment; the gesture of repudiation reasserts a link to previous generations.

Indeed, Lawrence has not received due credit for his innovation in the presentation of human time as repetition and difference. The Brangwensaga continually differentiates, in structure and theme, between types of repetition. The great structural innovation of *The Rainbow* is scenic echoing. Moon scenes in each generation, for example,

keep the reader vividly aware of the different fates of the three generations.[1] The moon on the pond in "Moony" and the "small bright
moon" that signals "no escape" to Gerald prolong this echo through
Women in Love. Moreover, the characters debate the ideas that are
simultaneously structuring the narrative. When is repetition fruitful
continuation or reinvigoration, and when is it entrapment or de-
basement? If one desires to escape from repetition, what will maintain
one's sense of identity? In fact, these two tendencies in repetition are
folded into each other.

Genealogical concepts of history, like those dominating *The Rainbow,* are conveyed in biological and specifically paternal imagery. This
first sort of repetition ensures the perpetuation of the species and
society. The radical intent of Lawrence's Brangwensaga, however, is
to have the familial line of succession pass from fathers to daughters,
thereby offering, as one critic has noted, "a vastly richer heritage than
does the single one of male descent . . . in which the female half of the
family fails to transmit itself."[2] Incidentally, this emphasis on fathers
and daughters is convincing evidence that Lawrence did master the
oedipal feelings he re-created in *Sons and Lovers.* The conflict of
mothers and sons rarely recurs in Lawrence's fiction, replaced by the
struggle of daughters to break free from paternal domination. History
now progresses through daughters; so *Women in Love* opens with the
sisters working out the Brangwen destiny. As Birkin jokes later, the
Brangwen "battle-cry" is "Do you love me?—Yield knave, or die"
(328). This lateral movement coincides with the shift from begetting
to self-begetting, so that "birth" becomes merely a metaphor. *Women
in Love* does not contain childbearing of the sort that betokens personal
or social renewal. Pussum thinks it "beastly" to be pregnant by Halliday, while Mrs. Crich, acting like a modern Medea, warns her assem-
bled children in the presence of her husband's corpse, "Don't let it
happen again!"—a cry of almost Delphic ambiguity that certainly
seems a warning against one sort of modern marriage.

This "strange, wild command" by Mrs. Crich epitomizes the
response to the second kind of repetition. According to Karl Marx,

repetition may be a parody of the filial relationship, producing "a disguised quasi-monstrous offspring, that is farce or debased language, rather than a handsome copy of the precursor or parent."[3] This second form exposes the ironies within language. "Probably," writes Edward Said, "the disparity between one version and its repetition increases, since repetition cannot long escape the ironies within it."[4] In *Women in Love*, repetition degenerates into farce or horror in modern times, entrapping rather than freeing. For example, it is a cause of claustrophobic terror to Gudrun that she can never escape the "eternal repetition" of her days and that Gerald, the deus ex machina, cannot save her. Fearing the future with Gerald, whose kisses resemble the "mechanical twitching" of clock time, she lives only in moments of physical abandon or fantasies of disruption, as in her game with Loerke of imagining "some mocking dream of the destruction of the world" (551).

The Crich family saga presents the pathos of paternity in the modern world, an ironic reversal of the woman-empowered, matrilineal progress of the Brangwens. The marriage of Mr. and Mrs. Crich is interdestructive, sending her mad and bleeding him of strength. At the wedding of one daughter, Mrs. Crich reveals the artificiality of marriage or even biology as the basis of the family. To her sons-in-law, whose names she cannot remember, she would like to say, "I am not your mother, in any sense" (73). Her own children remain almost indistinguishable, so far as arousing maternal feeling, from those of another woman. The Crich "family failing" of being "bad at living" and unable to "put a thing right, once it has gone wrong" (275, 252), announced by Gerald, leads to the failure of the father's paternalism toward his workers. Then Gerald's reorganization of the mines on inhuman principles enacts in public his involvement in his father's death, a "seeing through" or "dealing" that has implications of parricide.

This ironic revaluation of inheritance culminates in "Death and Love." The adventure of transforming the mines, of exercising his will power over matter and men, has led to Gerald's exhaustion rather than to replenishment in the Brangwen manner. Like a deus ex machina suffering entropy, Gerald must seek "reinforcements" or continue to bleed in the spiritual equivalent of his father's horribly slow death. In this extremity he turns to Gudrun, ignoring his mother's hysterical warning about marriage à la Crich, walking like a somnambulist to the Brangwen home via the graveyard, and arriving in Gudrun's room with shoes and pants smeared with mud from his father's grave. During their sexual consummation, Gudrun resents his regression to child-hood: "Like a child at the breast, he cleaved intensely to her, and she could not put him away" (431). Once Gudrun withdraws the emotional reinforcements, all of Gerald's energy and drive—his "go"—can only postpone eventual collapse. His final words, uttered before he wanders off to freeze, the weary "I didn't want it, really," recall as they fulfill his mother's curse. His death in a "shallow pot," "curled up" in the fetal position, may also recall Anton Skrebensky curled on the beach where he has retreated from Ursula's "fierce beaked harpy's kiss," or, further back, the positive, precursory image of Tom Brangwen "ceas[ing] to coil on himself" after meeting Lydia Lensky in the first generation of *The Rainbow*. Given the Crich family history, it is hardly surprising to discover that Lawrence abandoned the idea of concluding with a chapter in which, one year after the events of "Snowed Up," Gudrun writes to Ursula from Germany to report the birth of Gerald's son. Having discredited genealogy as an insurer of progress, Lawrence could not resurrect Gerald.

The prevalence of orphans as heroes in nineteenth-century fiction, such as Pip in *Great Expectations* or Jude Fawley in *Jude the Obscure*, has been discussed by Peter Brooks. He observes that "the parentless protagonist frees an author from struggle with pre-existing authorities, allowing him to create afresh all the determinants of plot within his text."[5] We have noted orphans in Lawrence's fiction and Ursula's breaking of family ties in *The Rainbow*. This rupture, a given in *Women in Love*, measures a difference between Lawrence's treatment of family history and that of nineteenth-century novelists. *Jude the Obscure* and *The Rainbow* have been astutely compared on this ground: "Whereas it is central to Hardy's purpose to show that Sue [Bridehead]'s tragedy is, in large measure, due to her failure to come to terms with a history at once public and private, it is central to Lawrence's purpose to reveal Ursula Brangwen's triumph as having behind it precisely that sense of history, but being able to find its climax in vision, which enables her to transcend her past. The generations of history give way to the regeneration of the individual."[6] Though this comparison highlights the celebration of transcendence, it does not recognize that the "regeneration of the individual" in Lawrence always accompanies an urgent desire to regenerate mankind. Indeed, Lawrence had conceived the Brangwensaga as a "re-sourcing" of art to make it "more the joint work of man and woman." Men and women must have the courage to reveal themselves to each other, thereby "gaining great blind knowledge and suffering and joy, which it will take a big further lapse of civilisation to exploit and work out."[7] But the creation of a utopian history is more speculative than the continuation through modification of generational history—a predicament or challenge that is debated throughout *Women in Love* and left hanging in the partly tragic, partly comic endings. Nevertheless, as the comparison with Hardy suggests, discontinuity is the rule in *Women in Love*. Paternity is a fiction, as we have been forewarned in the first and last generations of *The Rainbow*. Anna Lensky Brangwen can dethrone the Brangwen patriarch, her stepfather, by asserting "*You* are not my father—my father is dead."[8] And Skrebensky seeks shelter from the frightening truths of female sexuality and the "unknown" of the universe in the safe, patriarchal structures of marriage, the army, and colonial rule.

In the transition from *The Rainbow* to *Women in Love,* then, paternity becomes one of the preexisting authorities with which the Brangwen sisters must struggle, a fiction that no longer serves individual growth. Ursula escapes the hand of the past by fleeing her father's brutality and then questioning whether she can be the same person who visited her grandfather, Tom Brangwen, at the Marsh farm. Birkin thinks that Ursula's father, Will Brangwen, cannot be a "parent" and that her "spirit" has come from the "unknown" rather than a human "ancestor."

To repudiate paternity and the past, however, raises the problem of identity in a variety of tonalities. Hermione, the character most entrenched in a social identity, tries to kill Birkin because he is capable of slipping through the net of identity like a "chameleon" or "changer." One reason Birkin can change identity is that, like the outsider Loerke, he is an orphan. "Prologue" gave Birkin a university but not a family background, and the published novel supplies only a vestige of patrimony in the legacy of an annual stipend of 200 pounds sterling or 900 dollars (increased to 400 pounds in a second edition), which allows him to resign his position and encourage Ursula to do the same. Ursula considers Birkin's orphanhood a godsend, the fulfillment of her wish for a son of God who, having lived before Adam and Eve, is not encumbered by parents and antecedents. So Birkin comes to symbolize for Ursula the ideal of self-begetting, a utopian future made possible by "a bath of pure oblivion, a new birth, without any recollections or blemish of a past life" (502). Ursula has searched for someone who could assume the patriarchal authority of her grandfather Tom but has previously found only Skrebensky, a false incarnation. This failure in *The Rainbow* lends plausibility to her conflicted feelings in *Women in Love:* hostility toward men, fear of the lack of a man, and the gradual investing of hope in Birkin.

Thus the double novel conducts a debate on the varied images of time and the possibility that time may have an end but no redemption. One critic has distinguished three general conceptions of time in realistic fiction:

> (1) the cyclical conception, more common to primitive man, Eastern philosophies, and the pre-Socratic philosophers, the last of whom Lawrence read avidly in 1915;
> (2) the linear conception of Hebrew tradition, emphasizing beginnings and the presence of God through generations;
> (3) the linear conception of Christian tradition, emphasizing the end or *telos*, which retrospectively gives meaning to history.[9]

It could be argued that the first and second conceptions characterize both the Brangwens in *The Rainbow* and the novel's composition—a search for origins, generational progress toward a promised land, and historical renewal imaged in the cycles of nature. Then, to explain the crisis of a world war, *Women in Love* adds an urgent concern with the third conception of time but always in a dialectical manner. The characters debate questions of "fate" versus "accident." Did Gerald's killing of his brother simply happen, or does it reveal a murderous impulse in Gerald and a death wish in the Criches? Do people want anything different from what they get? And can change or rebirth come out of us or only after us?

> "If it is the end, then we are of the end—fleurs du mal if you like. If we are fleurs du mal, we are not roses of happiness, and there you are."
> "But I think I am," said Ursula. "I think I am a rose of happiness."
> "Ready-made?" he asked ironically.
> "No—real," she said, hurt.
> "If we are the end, we are not the beginning," [Birkin] said.
> "Yes, we are," she said. "The beginning comes out of the end." (239)

Critics tend to choose sides. To Frank Kermode, who sides with Birkin, biblical apocalypse provides the "radical type" of the novel.[10] But Ursula will not be shouted down; and as a Brangwen she knows both the "hideous actuality" of mankind and the likelihood of rebirth, the power of continuity as against apocalyptic disruption. The novel keeps its options open.

9

Social Reality

Just as the family history of the Brangwens has been disrupted by
the time *Women in Love* opens, so too the relationship between the
Brangwens and social reality is strained. Both sisters are estranged
from ordinary society. To Gudrun, the countryside is "defaced" and
the people "meaningless" or "ghoulish." The opening of *The Rainbow*
presents an image of social harmony in which Brangwens look up to
the vicar and the squire's family at Shelley Hall, who represent "the
wonder of the beyond," but the opening of *Women in Love* reverses
that perspective and breaks links between classes. Lawrence's myth of
history locates the source of breakdown in the rise of industrialism,
which turns all classes into servants of the machine. In *Women in Love*
the upper classes, both monied and professional, look down on the
"watchful, underworld faces" of the working-class women who, in
turn, give way "grudgingly" and remark cuttingly on the fashionable
dress of Gudrun ("What price the stockings?"). Hermione Roddice,
whose wealth is inherited, her brother Alexander, who is a Conserva-
tive member of Parliament, and their guests at the manor house, Breadalby, have no knowledge of workers. Mr. Crich, the plutocrat whose
new money keeps Great Britain and its overseas empire afloat, assuages

52

a guilty conscience by listening to the melodrama of poverty from miners whose wages he and the other owners hold down and by doling out cakes and milk to the children of striking miners. Having strongly opposed her husband's paternalism, Mrs. Crich has gone mad from suppressed fury. Their son and heir, Gerald, fully mechanizes the mining, ignoring the hatred this inspires in his workers because he knows that they too accept the new order. The godhead of the machine now forms a perverse bond between classes.

The professional classes are no less estranged from the workers. Will Brangwen found a "purposive" self as handicraft instructor in the second generation of *The Rainbow*, thereby connecting the Brangwens to "the great human endeavour" and gaining for them "a new vigour."[1] But he has become "obsolete" in the eyes of his daughters by the time of *Women in Love*, some fifteen years later. His interaction with the working classes, whose children he teaches at school, is not dramatized, and his daughters reject his notions of home and marriage even more decisively than Gerald rejects his father's relationship with the workers. Gudrun's response to the social reality of Beldover is highly ambivalent. She wants the "sordid" women who jeer at her arty clothes to be "annihilated." Yet she is drawn to the teeming life of the colliers, titillated by the sexual admiration of the miners, and attracted by Gerald because he is the master collier. Eventually, she rejects Gerald and the worlds of labor and politics that he dominates in favor of the expatriate life of an artist and *Glücksritter*, or adventurer.

Ursula is bewildered by the chasm between social classes. Her numbness or ineffectuality in the face of widening divisions makes better sense if we have read in *The Rainbow* that she has tried to cross class barriers. Ursula responds with sympathy to workers as diverse as a bargeman, taxi driver, and farmer despite the snobbish disapproval of her lover from the ruling classes, Anton Skrebensky. She also defends the miners in Wiggiston against the cynicism of her Uncle Tom; tries, though fails, to make personal contact with working-class children as a schoolmistress at Brinsley Street School; rejects escape from the Midlands through marriage to Anton, who moves in the world of country-house parties and will return to a career as military officer in colonial India; and, finally, envisions a future in which workers will be freed from the "prison" that encloses all mankind, as, through her miscarriage, she has been freed from the "compression" of Anton's world.

By recalling Ursula's personal history from *The Rainbow*, we can empathize with her initial state of being "inured to this violation of a dark, uncreated, hostile world" in *Women in Love*. The misunderstanding of Lawrence's social vision that can arise when *Women in Love* is severed from *The Rainbow* is illustrated by Joyce Carol Oates's remark that the novel shows a "total absence of concern for community" that is "distinctly un-English" and the result of a lack of "connection between one generation and the next."[2] Oates contrasts this alleged absence with the concern for community in James Joyce's *Ulysses* as projected through Leopold Bloom, who "yearns for community but is denied it." By omitting *The Rainbow* from her account of *Women in Love*, Oates misunderstands the myth of history Lawrence has been unfolding. For example, Oates misreads cynicism as traditionalism in Gudrun's late, capricious defense of home ("the old connection with the world—father and the rest of us . . . England") against Ursula's belief in the "other self, that belongs to a new planet" (533). The point is not that Ursula has come to endorse Birkin's desire to seek a new world; after all, she has taken the initiative in forcing Birkin to break his ties with Hermione's world and to flee the "unnatural" cold of the Alps for Italy. The point is rather that Gudrun speaks in insincere clichés, having already shown that she has no faith in social connections. She is repelled by the idea of marrying Gerald because he represents a maddeningly repetitive social life. The good sense in her opinion that "the only thing to do with the world, is to see it through" (534) should appear cynical or perhaps sinister, like Gerald's obstinacy in "seeing through" both the death of his father and his "blasting" affair with Gudrun herself (536). In contrast, Ursula's defense of the "unknown" continues the quest motif of *The Rainbow*.

In comparison to the varied life of *The Rainbow*—including farmers and workers of the land who congregate in market towns, miners in their raw new towns, workers with cultural pretensions, teachers, the children of a rapidly urbanizing England, liberated women, career soldiers, the bourgeoisie in country houses—the world of *Women in Love* is represented by three classes: aristocrats and plutocrats, teachers and bohemian artists, and workers. Catherine Carswell reports a conversation with Lawrence in which he defended this new focus:

> When [Lawrence] gave me the MS [of *Women in Love*] to read, I asked him why he must write of people who were so far removed from the general run, people so sophisticated and "artistic" and spoiled, that it could hardly matter what they did or said? To which he replied that it was only through such people that one could discover whither the general run of mankind . . . was tending. There, at the uttermost tips of the flower of an epoch's achievement, one could already see the beginning of the flower of putrefaction which must take place before the seed of the new was ready to fall clear.[3]

This rationale has elicited countercharges that Lawrence erred in locating the viewpoint in "characters so estranged from any community" that the novel cannot be comprehensive.[4] Such criticism loses much of its force when the two volumes are read together. Lawrence's rationale for *Women in Love* might serve for classical drama, which treats of the deeds of the highborn and all-powerful, the "tips of the flower of an epoch's achievement." The result is less comprehensiveness in social portraiture but greater coherence, so that, for example, "Breadalby" becomes a cross-section of bourgeois society. When Hermione as "priestess" of the occasion attacks Birkin with murderous intent, her social world stands accused of issuing perversely in death rather than life. Gerald, whom Birkin introduces to Pussum as "a soldier, explorer, and Napoleon of industry," seems to have his finger on the pulse of social England. The Crich family occupies a place similar to that of Mrs. Hardy, the squire's wife in the opening of *The Rainbow*, whose family history provides the Brangwen women with "their own Odyssey enacting itself." When a Crich daughter, Diana, is drowned in Willey Pond, "the colliery people felt as if this catastrophe had happened directly to themselves" (258).

Ursula is neither repelled nor secretly attracted by the life of the working classes. She is a pragmatist, tempered but not made cynical by the results of social division in both workers and masters. Whereas Gudrun exercises her artist's eye to reduce the complexity of people so as to be "finished" with them, Ursula keeps an open mind. In "A Chair," for example, she criticizes Birkin's nostalgia for Jane Austen's England: "It was materialistic enough. . . . I'm sick of the beloved past" (444). Then she extends sympathy to the young couple that must get married. Just as she earlier reassures Gudrun that the working-class women at the wedding are "all right," here she convinces Birkin that making a home is "right" for the working-class couple though not for themselves. When she offers the chair as a gift, however, she arouses suspicion. Birkin must rescue her. Class division remains the condition of England, despite brief moments of communication.

Fissures run within as well as between classes. Although language ideally bridges gaps, here it often works at cross-purposes. Conversations frequently end in mockery or abuse. A "pause of enmity," "mystic hate," and "contempt" follow debates between Birkin and Gerald. Hermione provokes and suffers from Birkin's blistering attacks. Gerald and Gudrun mock Birkin's notions of marriage. The characters can't decide what sort of faith to put in language or what demands to make of it. Gudrun dismisses the topic of home and marriage with the judgment, "What is it all but words!" (56) but later asks Birkin's opinion about the fate of England as though his words were an "instrument of divination" (487). One of the causes of tragedy is that, to the end, the characters cannot agree on the meaning of the most basic words: home, marriage, love. Birkin's last words to Gerald are, "I've loved you as well as Gudrun"—to which Gerald replies, "Have you? Or do you think you have?" (536).

10

Structure and Characterization

Lawrence's practice is dramatic in a precise sense. A novel may be called dramatic to signify that it contains vivid, scenic action or, as F. R. Leavis says, that it is "all significant life; not a scene, episode, image or touch but forwards the organized development of the theme."[1] In this second sense Lawrence's novels are "dramatic poems." Moreover, as the comparisons of novels to plays in *Study of Thomas Hardy* show, Lawrence thought of dramatic form on the analogy of a Greek play in which the tragedy arises from the conflict "between the great, single, individual forces in the nature of Man."[2] Greek drama presents man's actions as caused primarily by his own nature rather than the social law. Its example reveals the imbalance of so-called realistic fiction, which overemphasizes the shaping of character by social circumstance, the mere "objects we shine upon." In Lawrence's judgment, the leading Edwardian novelists—H. G. Wells, Arnold Bennett, and John Galsworthy—offer documentary fictions in which characters who lack a "real being" are victims of their possessions and social conventions. By contrast the "explosive" and "quite unreasonable" actions of Thomas Hardy's characters are manifestations of a "real, vital, potential self." In short, Lawrence conceived of his artistic task as a reassertion of the instinctual self in the shaping of our fates. As he stated in the foreword to *Women in Love:* "The creative, spontaneous soul sends forth its promptings of desire and aspiration in us. These promptings are our true fate, which is our business to fulfil. A fate dictated from outside, from theory or from circumstance, is a false fate."[3] Consequently, the emphasis falls more on character than fate in the form of accident or society. The narrative strips away masks of socially recognizable personality by which the depths of character are often disguised.

It has been argued that "*The Golden Bowl* deliberately incurs many of the formal limitations of a play."[4] That comment also provides a key to the narrative strategy of *Women in Love.* Just as we are accustomed to seeing the gesture of action on the Greek or Elizabethan stage as directly symbolic of character, so in *Women in Love* we are conditioned to see character creating its own destiny in a series of symbolic scenes. Instead of the historical arcs of *The Rainbow, Women in Love* proceeds through counterpointed scenes that may appear unexpected or even random but turn out to be inevitable on a deeper level. The narrative rhythm develops through what have been called "explosive self-objectifications."[5] Thus Gudrun watches while Gerald subdues the Arab mare at the railroad crossing in "Coal-Dust." Then she returns the challenge by intimidating Gerald's bullocks and striking a "first blow" in "Water-Party." Finally in "Rabbit" they come together as "initiates" while throttling Bismarck. Repeated ritual gestures link the scenes: Gudrun cries out in a voice like a seagull at critical moments; Gerald's reaction to her challenge in "Rabbit" echoes that in "Water-Party": "He felt again as if she had hit him across the face." In such scenes animals stand as symbolic surrogates, dramatic objects toward which the warring partners direct partly unconscious feelings. This seesaw rhythm foreshadows their unequal consummation in "Death and Love," which contrasts with the "equilibrium" achieved by Birkin and Ursula in "Excurse," setting a course of destructive passion that culminates in attempted murder and suicide. What Lawrence said of *Oedipus Rex* describes the novel's narrative rhythm: "It is terrible in its accumulation—like a big wave coming up—and then crash!"[6]

In its structuring of action and relevation of character, *Women in Love* is pervasively dramatic. It relies on prophetic equivocation leading to a tragic reversal. As in Shakespeare's *Macbeth,* a play of prophecy, the future is felt in the instant, even though the participants fail to act until it is too late to avert disaster.[7] All try to divine the future by reading the equivocal signs of the present and past. Mrs. Crich is a modern Cassandra; her weird hints that Gerald is "missing" and "hysterical," together with allusions to the accidental killing of his brother, suggest a fatality in Gerald. Following Gudrun's slap and promise to strike the "last" blow, for example, Gerald is ominously described as someone who "killed his brother when a boy, and was set apart, like Cain" (238). Both he and Gudrun seem half aware of these equivocations. Gudrun's "keen transport" at first sight of Gerald contains a warning, "His totem is the wolf," that proves prophetic in the Alps as she struggles "in his power—the wolf" (553). Gerald's thoughts as he awaits his father's death become self-fulfilling: "And then you realize that [death] was there all the time" (408).

Lawrence plunges the reader into the middle of things. Family history becomes an expression, rather than a cause, of character. When a sketch of Gerald's childhood, education, and manner of succeeding his father is given in "The Industrial Magnate," halfway through the novel, it confirms aspects of his character already presented in "Diver" and "Coal-Dust." The innovation is striking if we recall the concern for historical antecedence in a Victorian novel like *Middlemarch* or, indeed, Lawrence's own *Sons and Lovers.* A reader accustomed to this realist practice might object that there has been no time to establish the characters of Gudrun or Ursula or Hermione and that, therefore, their sudden apprehensions of Gerald and Birkin in "Sisters" are not wholly intelligible on first reading. For a similar reason, one critic objected that in the opening of Tolstoy's *Anna Karenina* Anna falls in love with Vronsky while she is still "incompletely rendered": "If she is so soon to be seen at this pitch of exaltation, it is essential that her life should be fully shared by the onlooker."[8] From such a perspective, Gudrun's violent "possession" on first seeing Gerald will seem unprepared, as, indeed, will Hermione's "devastating hopelessness" when she finds that Birkin has not arrived for the wedding, or Ursula's bitter weeping after witnessing the argument between Birkin and Hermione in "Class-Room." One might meet this objection by noting that the background to Hermione's situation is given in "Prologue" or that the bruise left by Ursula's affair with Skrebensky had always been a part of the novel's conception. But that line of defense would misrepresent Lawrence's special brand of psychological realism.

11

Language, Modern Painting, and the War

All theories of ultimate origin are only ways of better defining what
followed.

—John Berger[1]

When Edward Garnett complained that *The Rainbow* did not contain
the sort of "realistic" characterization he admired in *Sons and Lovers,*
Lawrence defended his new conception of character:

That which is physic—non-human, in humanity, is more interesting
to me than the old-fashioned human element—which causes one
to conceive a character in a certain moral scheme and make him
consistent. . . . I don't care so much about what the woman *feels*—
in the ordinary usage of the word. That presumes an *ego* to feel
with. I only care about what the woman *is* . . . as a phenomenon
(or as representing some greater, inhuman will), instead of what
she feels according to the human conception. . . . You mustn't look
in my novel for the old stable ego of the character. There is another
ego, according to whose action the individual is unrecognizable,
and passes through, as it were, allotropic states which . . . are states
of the same radically-unchanged element. (Like as diamond and
coal are the same pure single element of carbon. The ordinary novel

61

would trace the history of the diamond—but I say "diamond, what!
This is carbon." And my diamond might be coal or soot, and my
theme is carbon.)[2]

During work on *The Sisters* it was natural for Lawrence to define his
aim in terms of a woman's psychology. Living in Italy he had been
perusing the manifestos and paintings of the Italian Futurists. Like
other literary modernists, such as Virginia Woolf and Ernest Heming-
way, Lawrence used the analogy of modern painting when describing
the momentous "change" in human nature that took place shortly
before or during the world war. According to Woolf, human nature
changed in 1910, the date of the famous Postimpressionist exhibition
in London, of which Paul Cézanne was the hero. For Lawrence the
war seemed an artistic climacteric. People had felt too deeply to be
fooled any longer by popular realism. There would be an audience for
novels that, like Cézanne's paintings, were "objective" in the sense of
delving beneath the surface or "diamond" of character to the essential
"carbon" while avoiding the visual cliché. The letter's curious diction
of chemico-mechanistic process reflects the influence of the Futurists.
Though he quoted their manifestos in 1914 and painted several pictures
in a futuristic style (for example, *Flight Back into Paradise*), Lawrence
did not accept their "glorification of the machine-world as the basis
for the new art."[3] Indeed, he criticized the Futurists for pursuing the
"purely male or intellectual or scientific line," whereas he believed the
re-sourcing of art must come from the joint work of man and woman.
What Lawrence did see in their work was the clue to "dealing with the
precise phase of alienation which . . . had now come upon men."[4]

The outbreak of the war only a few months later showed the
aptness of the Futurist vision to the modern condition. In the dazzling
ferocity of Ursula's pitched battles with Skrebensky, for example, Lawrence invented a linguistic analogue of Futurist painting. The moon
scenes in chapters 11 and 15 of *The Rainbow* contain a vocabulary of
physical processes applied with shocking effect to human emotions.
To Skrebensky, who has tried to "net" her in the dance, Ursula appears

"cold," "corrosive," a "blade" of destruction. She has the fierce clarity of the great "moon-conflagration" as well as the "whitish-steely" fires of the corn stacks, whereas he appears as "dross," "soft iron" or "inert."[5] Though the extreme sensuality of these love scenes has often been remarked, the relevance of Futurist technique to characterization has been missed. The link between psychology and history provides a clue. These amorous battles are lacerating because, in fighting Skrebensky, Ursula is really fighting that part of her self that *is* he and the world he represents. When Anton flees her "fierce, beaked, harpy's kiss," Ursula lies rigid and crying, "cold, dead, inert." She has killed a part of herself. According to the imaginative logic, the world in the form of Ursula's social ego is hostile, entrenched, and must be fought to the death before the natural or "dark" self can come forth.

Futurist art and similar movements like Cubism, as in Loerke's frieze based on Mark Gertler's painting, *Merry-Go-Round,* express a condition of modern alienation or disruption between the sexes and between man and nature. As an accurate depiction of the mechanized world that all modern characters have internalized, however, they could not serve to represent a liberating or renovating passion. Consequently, Lawrence's futuristic verbal effects are dystopian, not utopian—more appropriate in an ironic fable of a scientifically controlled society like Aldous Huxley's *Brave New World* (1932) than in a socialist romance about the future like William Morris's *News from Nowhere* (1891), which Lawrence read in his youth.

Consider, for example, a moment near the tragic climax of *Women in Love,* when Gudrun's love for Gerald has turned into a compound of fear and willfulness. In revision she becomes a futuristic Eve: "She looked at Gerald [He looked like a fruit made to eat. He was her apple of knowledge.] <He was wonderful like a piece of radium to her.> She felt she could [set her teeth in him and eat him to the core] <consume herself and know *all,* by means of this fatal, living metal.>[6] It is no coincidence that skiing and sledding, "the ecstasy of physical motion" that Gudrun calls "the complete moment of . . . life," are described in the prose equivalent of Futurism; or that Gerald becomes absorbed in sports as an escape from failure in human relationships, whereas Birkin and Ursula flee the sheer speed and motion that is turning the English couples into "snow-creatures"; or, finally, that the frieze Loerke designs for a modern factory depicts the workers in a "frenzy of chaotic motion," controlled by the machine as are Gerald's miners. Verbal Futurism describes processes of dissolution or corruption that are both deplorable and, as we shall see, necessary. Dystopia must precede Utopia.

Primitive art, like Futurist painting, gave Lawrence metaphors for describing the fate of England. *Women in Love* reflects the fascination of Europe with primitive artifacts brought back from African colonies, as in, for example, Pablo Picasso's *Les Demoiselles d'Avignon.*[7] The West African woodcarvings in Halliday's flat are displayed alongside several paintings "in the Futurist manner." One carving, a statue of a naked woman in labor, provokes a conversation on art between Birkin and Gerald and later, in "Moony," becomes the object of Birkin's meditation on cultural decline. To Gerald the statue seems "obscene," while to Birkin it is high "art" because it expresses truthfully the African "culture of *physical* sensation." Since *obscene* carries traces of "inauspicious or ill-omened," as well as the more common "indecent," Gerald's comment raises the question of the relevance of primitive art to the condition of England. Gerald's objection that Birkin likes "things against yourself" is more accurate than he can know. When meditating in "Moony" Birkin comes to realize, as Gerald never does, that the degeneration symbolized in the African statue is "imminent" in himself and European culture. Then, as the tragic climax approaches, Gerald seems transformed into a primitive statue, his face looking "like a mask used in ghastly religions of the barbarians" (536). The imminent has arrived.

A myth of historical decline explains this aspect of Lawrence's linguistic practice, his reliance on certain modern paintings and artifacts. In remarks on Thomas Hardy's *Return of the Native,* for example, he expresses a faith in the connection between man and nature similar to the faith of the Romantic poets and the mood in which he began *The Rainbow:* "What is the real stuff of tragedy in the book? It is the Heath . . . the primitive primal earth, where the instinctive life heaves up . . . a great background, vital and vivid, which matters more than the people who move upon it."[8] The lives of Tom and Lydia in the first generation are perfectly mirrored in natural rhythms. The second generation of Will and Anna Brangwen, however, is not at home in either the Marsh or the modern world; so the language of natural cycles cannot fully express them. By the time he came to rewrite the novel in 1915, Lawrence had grasped the connection between the rise of industrial capitalism he was chronicling and the world war through which he was living. "The Child" chapter uses language similar to that in the letter on the Futurists because Will and Anna must indulge in a more extreme form of sexuality if they are to achieve rebirth or transcendence, as their parents had before them. When Will seduces a warehouse lass and then returns home a "strange man," his emotions are described like physical phenomena in futuristic verbs such as "absorb" and "fuse" or nouns such as "properties" and "activities."[9] Will and Anna must burn out the repressive social ego that is reflected in the war, as must Ursula later in battles with Skrebensky.

By the fictional time of *Women in Love,* the repressiveness of society and the social ego has worsened. Lawrence's vision grew more dire with each generation. Both the deathliness of sexuality and the need for what Birkin calls an "impersonal" relationship, "neither love nor passion," are desperately apparent. The natural rhythms of Marsh life have been destroyed, and modern society offers nothing in their place but the false pastoralism of Hermione's country estate or the mechanized horror of Beldover. As a linguistic consequence, there are few analogies by which to suggest the rebirth of personal and social life, whereas metaphors of death are abundant. Pussum and Halliday, like Gerald and Gudrun, swim in the "river of dissolution" or treat each other as machines. Just as mankind may have reached the end of its creative day, nature seems debilitated, overspread by industrialism and transformed by psychic anxiety. The attempts by Ursula and Birkin to overcome this estrangement from the natural world meet with mixed success. Bleeding from Hermione's violent blow with a rock, for example, Birkin escapes to the open country outside the park at Breadalby. There he conducts a private vegetation rite, flinging off his clothes and "saturating" himself with the touch of grass and tree. The experience is healing. He recognizes his falsity in castigating Hermione's world while remaining a part of it: "It was quite right of Hermione to want to kill him. What had he to do with her? Why should he pretend to have anything to do with human beings at all? . . . He knew where to plant himself, his seed;—along with the trees, in the folds of the delicious fresh-growing leaves. This was his . . . marriage place. The world was extraneous" (166). Having experienced a death to the "old ethic" of continuity through marriage or family, Birkin here reaches the predicament of Ursula at the end of *The Rainbow*. From atop the Sussex Downs, where she has gone alone to celebrate the "intercourse" between the "unabateable body" of the earth and the "changeful body" of the sky, Ursula weeps at the sight of a train that has "tunnelled all the earth," a symbol of modern disruption.[10] Like Birkin, she would prefer to plant herself on the downs, to "become a strong mound."

In counterpoint to Ursula's anguish at the alienation of man from nature, Gudrun relishes her role in the modern myth of industrialism, "like a new Daphne, turning not into a tree but a machine" (174). Arriving in the Tyrol, she is drawn to the antipastoral landscape. The cul-de-sac of a snowy valley, which resembles a "cradle" and the body of a woman, sends her into raptures. She cannot see the irony any more than Gerald can recognize that his love for her will end literally in the icy embrace of such a valley. For a time she amuses herself with visions of guiding Gerald to preeminence in the social or political world: "His instrumentality appealed so strongly to her, she wished she were God, to use him as a tool" (511). Then, as their affair degenerates into a battle of wills, they revel in the ecstasy of speed that Loerke celebrates in his granite frieze as the condition of industrial man.

Thus language and setting perfectly match. According to the Futurists, modern life was a "vortex," a life of "steel, fever, pride and headlong speed"—terms that apply precisely to the tragic finale of

Gerald and Gudrun's love affair. The Futurist manifesto of 1910 also asserts that "motion and light destroy the material nature and look of solid bodies."[11] Whether skiing in the blinding glare of the mountains or making love that "cuts" and "blasts," Gerald and Gudrun create a vortex in which their love dissolves. It is what Birkin earlier calls the "destructive frost mystery" (331), a process of cultural as well as individual degeneration. The games of sublimated destructiveness that Gudrun and Loerke play, like those of Hermione and her guests at Breadalby, are yet another sterile ritual of modern life.

12

Animals and Humans

Far back, far back in our dark soul the horse prances.
—Lawrence, *Apocalypse*[1]

That the rituals of modern life are deathly rather than life giving is also registered in the treatment of animals. According to the anthropologists Lawrence read, Greek drama had its origins in religious rituals associated with the cult of Dionysos that included animals as participants and victims: "Dionysos appears freely as a snake, bull, he-goat and lion."[2] In Lawrence's fiction, horses, bullocks, rabbits, snakes, and other animals embody universal energies that modern man neglects or represses at his peril. Animal images from Euripides' tragedies haunt *Women in Love*. The image of Agave and her Maenads rending the cattle in *The Bacchae*, for example, returns in "Water-Party" as does the image of Hippolytus and his horses in "Coal-Dust." Indeed, the Brangwensaga embodies a myth of what John Berger calls the "cultural marginalization" of animals. According to Berger, animals in preindustrial societies were imagined to possess a secret power specifically addressed to man. Their function included magic and sacrifice as well as labor and food. Lacking human language, animals offered a curious, parallel companionship to man, who is otherwise lonely as a species. In sum, the relationship was paradoxical: animals were "subjected *and* worshipped, bred *and* sacrificed."[3]

Berger's analysis resembles the historical myth in Lawrence. In an essay called "Pan in America," Lawrence states that man has needed the "qualities of every living thing," including rock, tree, bear, deer, and eagle.[4] The preindustrial state corresponds to the first-generation Brangwens in *The Rainbow* for whom "it was enough that they helped the cow in labour, or ferreted the rats from under the barn, or broke the back of a rabbit with a sharp knock of the hand."[5] It is natural that Tom Brangwen, Ursula's grandfather, should comfort his young stepchild Anna during her mother's labor by taking her with him to feed the cattle. Ever since Descartes split man into soul and body, however, animals have been considered soulless, to be used as machines or raw materials like the workers in the Crich mines. This myth explains why Gerald's treatment of mare, bullock, and rabbit prefigures his treatment of the workers or Gudrun; why Gudrun swoons at the sight of Gerald abusing the mare; and why Gudrun and Gerald feel "initiate" after nearly breaking the neck of Bismarck the rabbit. Animals in *Women in Love* are exploited or transformed into artifacts like Loerke's futuristic bronze statue of a stallion, "stretched in a kind of start . . . rigid with pent-up power," that expresses the brutality of its creator. In either use, their mystery has disappeared.

At the same time that animals have been "marginalized," however, they have become central in our dreams: "the life of a wild animal becomes an ideal . . . internalized as a feeling surrounding a repressed desire."[6] Isn't this the situation of Ursula at the end of *The Rainbow* when she is visited by the horses? The horses are both actual creatures and projections of her repressed desire—"mortal and immortal," in Berger's terms. In *St. Mawr* (1925) the horse comes from a "prehistoric twilight" where "all things loomed phantasmagoric, all on one plane," just as the horses suddenly "loom in the rain" and confront Ursula.[7] And in *Apocalypse* (1929) Lawrence celebrated the horse as the symbol of "potency and power of movement, of action" in man, noting that in the Bible the sons of God who knew the daughters of men were said to have the members of horses.[8] Gerald Crich mesmerizes Gudrun while subduing the mare and then seduces her with "superhuman force" (493). But his maleness, his stallionlike energy, becomes distasteful and threatening to her. She prefers the homosexual artist Loerke who has "some understanding of a woman." It is a tragic irony that Gerald's frozen corpse reminds Birkin of a "dead stallion" (582).

The mystery of animals and the ideal of human nature unimprisoned by society have disappeared. We will not get them back by the anthropomorphism of Hermione Roddice, who talks to a stag as if he were a naughty boy or tells stories of a male swan's amorous misadventure, or by ascribing human motives to cats so as to prove a sexist argument, as Birkin does and Ursula protests in "Mino." "How stupid anthropomorphism is," thinks Ursula, because it rejects the "uncanny" in animals. Indeed, at the nadir of her fortunes in "Moony," she detests adults and feels love only for children or, best of all, any animal who, like herself, is "single and unsocial . . . magical" (320).

Many of Lawrence's subsequent stories and tales—*The Fox, St. Mawr*, "The Rocking Horse Winner," *The Virgin and the Gipsy*—explore the consequences of man's estrangement from the animal without and within him. The pathetic boy in "The Rocking Horse Winner" projects onto horses his repressed desire for a naturalness in life, riding a wooden hobbyhorse, which he should have outgrown, in order to predict a winner and thereby satisfy his mother's craving for money. In this ironic fable the horse has an oracular function but the boy dies. Only on the borders of the modern world can humans occasionally reestablish a living connection to animals and their own humanity.

The Fox (1921) extends techniques of characterization that appear in *Women in Love*. Henry Grenfell, the young man who intrudes into the female household, succeeds in winning the love of March because, by shooting the fox, he captures its mana or supernatural force. March has subliminally willed Henry to rescue her, having found in the presence of the fox a mysterious release from the tension of her life. This split in her consciousness between the "keen and observant" and an "odd, rapt state," which the fox and then Henry heal, is conveyed in paradoxical images of sight/blindness and knowledge/ unknown that recall *Women in Love*. March's sighting of the fox, for example, balances realism and myth. She feels instantly that "he knew her" and is spellbound, possessed. The dog-fox becomes "a settled effect in her spirit . . . not continuous, but always recurring." After Henry unexpectedly arrives, she identifies him with the fox, fusing the two planes of consciousness and "laps[ing] into the odour of the fox." When March judges Henry from the conventional viewpoint of her myopic friend, Banford, the young man seems an upstart. When they embrace, however, the beat of his heart feels "like something from beyond . . . signalling to her." Though Henry is keen-sighted like the fox, he does not "know" her in the everyday sense. Similarly, March goes with Henry "darkly" though she does not know who he is.[9]

   The Fox, then, embodies Lawrence's belief in the vivid relatedness between man and the living universe or, in short, his mythic realism. Animals are never presented in the likeness of man, but man appears in the likeness of animals; the universe is not anthropomorphized, but the boundaries of human consciousness are expanded. The simplified logic of passion in this tale builds on the complexities of the Brangwen-saga. How to live in the commonplace, drawing from one's source in the beyond that is also deep within one, is the problem that challenges all natural aristocrats. In one sense Tom Brangwen does not know Lydia any better after their years of wedded passion, though in another he knows her "altogether." Birkin articulates the paradox when he insists that he does not want to see Ursula's beauty. To her indignant protest, he replies: "I want to find you, where you don't know your own existence, the you that your common self denies utterly" (210). And Ursula agrees in Sherwood Forest that "She would have to touch him. To speak, to see, was nothing" (402). The true passion that gains for Ursula and Birkin "an inheritance of a universe of dark reality" is paradoxical; their knowledge of each other must be a death of knowl- edge. On the other hand, the paradox of sight/blindness may signal a failure to renew one's life. No character in the novel is more keen-sighted than Gerald, yet he is blind to his effect on people and blinded by the fearsome strain of his destructive affair with Gudrun. As he admits to Birkin, the extreme desirability of Gudrun "blasts your soul's eye . . . and leaves you sightless" (536). His blindness can be distinguished from that of Birkin and Ursula in Sherwood Forest by the fact that it is always a blindness to, never a blindness with, the other person. His "lapsing-out" leads to isolation and depletion rather than renewal through touch. Dionysos becomes Samson, his blindness self-inflicted and his death a barren tragedy. Similarly, Gudrun's trance of rapture at the sight of the "blind" valley in the Tyrol presages her estrangement from Gerald. In Gerald and Gudrun, then, the two planes of consciousness never fuse harmoniously, and this splitting is signaled by their abuse of horse or rabbit and their own transformation into sinister "snow-creatures" preying on each other.

13

Sight and Touch

Vision is the privileged faculty of perception in realist fiction. The nineteenth-century novelist often described his or her task in the metaphor of a mirror reflecting the surface of the world. Stendhal likened his novels to mirrors carried along a highroad, and a century later Joyce mocked this commonplace in *Ulysses* when Stephen Dedalus calls Irish art "the cracked looking-glass of a servant." Lawrence's habitual punning on sight/blindness or known/unknown has a revolutionary intent. The new "allotropic states" of character in *The Rainbow* require in readers "a deeper sense" than the eye of traditional realism.[1] This is why Cézanne is the preeminent modern painter. In "Introduction to These Paintings" (1929), Lawrence praises Cézanne for avoiding the "optical cliché" in his still lives and portraits of his wife and for thereby shattering "kodak" images of the self: "while he was painting the appleyness he was also deliberately painting *out* the so-called humanness, the personality, the 'likeness,' the physical cliché."[2] As always Lawrence links technique in art to conceptions of the self. His re-sourcing of art meant reasserting the primacy of the dark body over the reflective mind and the sense of touch over sight. When Birkin stones the moon's image on Willey Pond, he is attacking his own false ego or self-image as much as the "Syria Dea" or woman. Watching from the shadows, Ursula feels "spilled out," as though Birkin has been acting on her behalf too, shattering an image of herself in which she has been imprisoned. The action recalls Birkin's earlier attack on Hermione, whom he accuses of being imprisoned, like the Lady of Shalott, in the "mirror" of a fixed will or false consciousness. On that occasion he predicts that she will never become a spontaneous woman until her skull is "cracked like a nut." Hermione takes the suggestion and attempts to crack *his* skull.

In sum, Birkin's stoning of the moon completes a series of scenes in which the clash between the "old ego" and the new is suggested in the opposition of one metaphoric network (sight/will/knowledge/ bondage) to another (darkness/lapsing or dissolving/the unknown/freedom). The style of the stoning scene—like that of the dancing in "Water-Party" or wrestling in "Gladiatorial"—expresses psychic life in a literary analogue to a painting by the Futurists or Cézanne. It is prose aspiring to the condition of modern painting.

In Lawrence's mythic realism, consequently, the moments in which a character shapes his or her fate in accordance with the promptings of the deepest self are usually heralded by a "trance," "stupor," "spell," "swoon," or "possession." At such moments characters project their desire on the world or recognize a lover's true desire. These are moments of metamorphosis or mythic possession when landscape and character appear strange yet inevitable.

There can be very different reactions to such possession. When Gerald surprises Gudrun by stealing into her room, he seems "inevitable as a supernatural being" (428). Gudrun cannot send him away, for she recognizes in him "an apparition, the young Hermes" (429), the very god capable of accomplishing such a bold feat. Having previously wooed Gudrun in the guises of industrial deus ex machina and tamer of horse and bullock and rabbit, Gerald comes to her as Jove did to Leda or Europa. After their consummation, while Gerald sleeps on her breast, Gudrun feels "an ache of nausea," as though he were an intruder who had raped her. The sexual consummation renews Gerald, as we learn in images of touch such as "enveloping soft warmth" or "soothing flow of life" (430). For Gudrun, however, the aftermath is ambiguous; she lies awake, staring into the darkness, "destroyed" into consciousness. In the preceding chapter Birkin and Ursula consummate their mystic marriage deep in Sherwood Forest. Birkin has been metamorphosed into one of the "inhuman" sons of God, magically fulfilling Ursula's adolescent dream. His possession, unlike Gerald's, is unequivocally desired. The lovers see and know each other in ways that are paradoxically "never to be revealed" and that confirm the "death of knowledge." Like her Brangwen ancestors, Ursula inherits the "mystic body of reality" through touch.

This contrast between sight and touch may explain an aspect of the book that amused the early reviewers, what J. M. Murry called "the sedulous catalogues of unnecessary clothing," which he suggested are failed efforts to distinguish men and women who are really as "indistinguishable as octopods in an aquarium tank."[3] In fact, Lawrence scrupulously revised these catalogues, which have several apt thematic uses. They serve to contrast the peacock sisters, especially the bohemian Gudrun, with the plainly dressed, "dark" mining population. They are the sisters' means of lifting themselves above the environment in which both feel trapped. Their clothing makes an aesthetic statement and empowers them, especially Gudrun. Like the denizens of the Pompadour, readers are mesmerized by Gudrun's elegant outfits. Yet characters who place a high value on proper or arty dress like Gerald, Gudrun, and Hermione reveal an attachment to the visual and the surface as opposed to the tactile and the unknown. This implies a commitment to the social status quo and to the willpower needed to maintain a hierarchy of taste and class. Think of Gerald robing himself in a silk caftan after wrestling with Birkin, perhaps as a defense against the temptation to admit his love for Birkin; or of Gerald stealing into Gudrun's room wearing formal dinner clothes, so that in unfastening the pearl studs from his starched linen he makes the sound of pistol shots; or, in contrast, of Birkin and Ursula simply and silently throwing off their clothes in Sherwood Forest. Whereas Gudrun is unable to "lapse out" during sex or to sleep afterwards, Ursula and Birkin achieve a mutual "revelation of mystic otherness" that cannot be either seen or heard.

14

Dawn of the Gods: Mythic Realism

Gods haunt the world of *Women in Love*. Olympian deities such as Aphrodite, Artemis, Dionysos, Hebe, and Hermes consort with Judeo-Christian heroes and villains such as the sons of God in Genesis, Samson, and Cain. The Germanic god Loki and the mythical kings of the Nibelungs jostle primitive cult figures of the Magna Mater and Syria Dea. In addition to these apparitions, we may sense the presences of the divine king or scapegoat, characters from Greek drama such as Pentheus and Agave from *The Bacchae,* and figures of contemporary political and cultural legend such as Kaiser Wilhelm, Rupert Brooke, and Lady Ottoline Morrell. A traveler between worlds, Lawrence possessed an archaic sensibility and a gift for re-creating mythic experience, as we have seen in *The Fox.* Lawrence's imaginary borderland extends beyond class and geography to the "border line" of life and death, as he titled a later short story. Did he literally believe in gods and ghosts? He wrote ghost stories, such as "Glad Ghosts" or "The Border Line," and the mythic narrative of *The Escaped Cock.* A brief comparison with the practice of James Joyce and Thomas Hardy will put Lawrence's mythic realism into perspective.

Although this aspect of his art bears a superficial resemblance to what T. S. Eliot called the "mythical method" of James Joyce in *Ulysses*, Lawrence's vision is quite different—mythical in a re-creative rather than allusive sense. Eliot praised Joyce for contriving a "continuous parallel between contemporaneity and antiquity" as a way of countering modern "futility and anarchy."[1] As Joyce's title announces, Homer has come to Dublin, though not a single character from the *Odyssey* appears in *Ulysses* and the links between Joyce and Homer are parallels that never meet. In fact, Joyce places greater emphasis on those features of Dublin life and Irish character that do *not* coincide with Homer. Since the dominant technique is mock heroic, readers are always aware that Leopold Bloom as the "new womanly man" is not Ulysses nor his promiscuous wife, Molly, a faithful Penelope.

Nor does Lawrence's mythical method resemble that of Thomas Hardy, who strove for Greek effects in tragic novels like *The Return of the Native*. As Hardy's manuscripts reveal, he tried to create a tragic atmosphere by superimposing a classical frame of reference on a regional novel. Egdon Heath in remote Wessex is compared to various Greek underworlds, "Tartarus" or "Homer's Cimmerian land," and the tragic heroine Eustacia Vye is given a Homeric pedigree: "Where did her dignity come from? *By a latent vein from Alcinous' line, her father hailing from Phaecia's isle?*—or from Fitzaland and DeVere" (emphasis added).[2] But Hardy's technique, lacking the irony of Joyce's mock heroism, seems artificial in a realistic novel. Homer may have journeyed to Dublin, but he did not stop in Wessex.

Lawrence never worked in either manner. In fact, he deplored the applied classicism of Rupert Brooke, the English poet whose poetic style and early death in the war were transformed by politicians into the noble lie that Edwardian England resembled Homeric Greece. Brooke's sonnets, filled with pastoral images of England imitated from classical verse, were eulogized as patriotic in the face of German aggression. Brooke himself was so often compared to Apollo that he came to believe it, setting off for Europe "to kill my Prussian" and "mix a few sacred and Apollonian English ashes" with his fallen compatriots.[3] His sonnet, "The Dead," ends by asserting that "we have come into our heritage," which was not the Brangwens' heritage of renewed life. Lawrence saw the death wish through the style: "[Brooke] was slain by bright Phoebus shaft. . . . It is all in the saga . . . It is like a madness."[4] On the other hand, Lawrence never suffered the disillusionment of educated soldiers for whom the gods had died in the trenches of a world war. To one friend of Brooke and other fallen heroes, a visit after the war to the legendary sites of the Hellespont and Troy confirmed a mythic as well as personal loss: "The great Pan is dead, and the world of which he is the symbol; we can never recapture it."[5]

Yet Pan prances through Lawrence's fictional landscapes and flickers to life in Rupert Birkin. Consider the chapter "Class-Room." Although Ursula's curiosity is piqued by Birkin in "Sisters," she does not have a powerful "apprehension" of him there as her sister does of Gerald. Her moment comes in "Class-Room," when the school inspector unexpectedly pays her a visit: "She saw in the shaft of ruddy, copper-coloured light near her, the face of a man" (84). When Hermione arrives, Ursula witnesses a heated argument between the ex-lovers on the subject of knowledge and sensuality or, as Birkin puts it, "the vicious, mental-deliberate profligacy our lot goes in for" (94). But here, as throughout the novel, Ursula intuits another Birkin hidden beneath his declamatory style: "the powerful beauty of life itself, something like laughter, invisible and satisfying" (94). Suddenly she has a mythic vision of him as the god Pan: "Also the magic of his thighs had fascinated her: the inner slopes of his thighs. She could not say what it was. But there was a sense of richness and of strong, free liberty" (94).[6] From a solely realist perspective, a reader may wonder how Ursula can admire Birkin's thighs through his clothing and before they have become lovers. From a mythic perspective, however, Ursula has apprehended Pan beneath Birkin's conventional appearance. Earlier in *The Rainbow*, having become Skrebensky's lover, Ursula notices the "stiff goat's legs" almost hidden under the clothing of ordinary citizens.[7] In "A Chair," having become Birkin's lover, she has a similar vision of the young man who is a "mindless creature" of the towns but whose "legs would be marvelously subtle and alive, under the shapeless trousers" (446). Birkin later demonstrates the uncanny power of Pan, who is "more demon than god," while wrestling, dancing, and making love.[8] Dancing in the Reunionsaal, for example, he fascinates and frightens Ursula with the "licentious mockery" of his eyes and his strength like "black-magic." In bed afterwards she wonders that someone so "soulful" can also be so "unabashed and . . . bestial" (505). Just as Gerald appears to Gudrun as northern god, Hermes, and sinister wolf, so Birkin appears to Ursula as biblical son of God and pagan Pan. The epiphanies, or appearances of gods, reflect different facets of complex characters.

The gods remain as real as our desires and dreams. Lawrence adapts techniques and motifs from mythology or Greek drama because he believes that something in nature lies behind the literary manifestations of mythic metamorphosis, something that erupts into culture in various forms of revolutionary desire. Rather than repeat with ironic inflection myths from previous literature, as Joyce and Eliot do, Lawrence creates his own myth-saturated realism. We may understand this mythic impulse by remembering that narrative realism exists in a continuum running from naturalism to fairy tale or myth, from Emile Zola to the Brothers Grimm. Realism cannot do without either impulse. Though he advocated scientific objectivity in the naturalist novel, Zola wove myths into his own novels.[9] Joyce imposed a mythic order on *Ulysses* but included a chaotic wealth of detail that he dubbed "Dublin street furniture"—names, addresses, local events, and newspaper cuttings. Lawrence too finds a place in the continuum. Even in his most fully mythic scenes, when events follow the uncanny logic of dreams, a residue of realistic motivation keeps the novel from turning into a myth. The abrupt shifts between comparative scenes prepare for self-objectifications that often involve the implied or direct appearance of a god. As one critic has remarked, *Women in Love* must be read as "half novel, half myth."[10]

A few examples, to be elaborated later, may be given now. Gudrun rushes on the bullocks and strikes Gerald across the face while thinking to herself, "Why *are* you behaving in this *impossible* and ridiculous manner?" (237). If we have read *The Golden Bough*, as Lawrence had, we may suspect that the bullocks stand for Gerald as sacrificial animals stood for divine kings who were ritualistically killed to ensure a rebirth of nature and power in primitive societies. At the novel's tragic climax, Gerald compares himself to a "victim that is torn open and given to the heavens" (543), confirming our suspicion that the scene in "Water-Party" is mythic as well as realistic. Hermione, the "priestess" of Breadalby, nearly achieves a "voluptuous consummation" by striking Birkin's skull with a ball of lapis lazuli but fails because her fingers deaden the blow. Does Ursula simply happen upon Birkin beside the pond in "Moony" or conjure him into existence as in a fairy tale or myth? She has wished for "something else out of the night," and the stoning dissipates her "old ego" as though on cue. Gerald appears to Gudrun as Hermes but makes the noise of pistol shots when unfastening his collar studs and next morning reminds Gudrun of a workman. At first sight Gudrun associates Gerald totemistically with a wolf; shortly before he attempts to strangle her, she fears falling prey to "his power [as] the wolf" (553). But Gerald's wolfish resolve weakens and, overcome by self-loathing, he kills himself.

Another way to explain this blend of myth and realism is to say that a clash between characters, what the Greeks called an *agon*, arises from the struggle within characters. The impression is created of a strong undertow of emotion in both individual and society that may flare into beneficent or destructive life. According to the metaphor of "allotropical" states, a character passes from the "diamond" of individual through class to mythic essence or "carbon," and then back again to social identity and individuality. Character is dissolved and reconstituted in a rhythm of explosive change and continuity that marks the entire Brangwensaga. As a consequence, the plot of *Women in Love* does not build to a single climax but instead proceeds through a series of startling minor climaxes.

15

Style

Lawrence is a prodigious stylist who invented new ways to evoke the "carbon" of character, but he never lost the realist's eye for a telling detail or the poet's facility with metaphor. His ability to project himself into foreign cultures and modes of being, which accounts for his success as a travel writer who captures the "spirit of place," is an extension of his artistic range at home. As the son of a miner he had what Henry James praised in Joseph Conrad's tales of Africa and the Far East— the authority of his materials. In the rigid class society of England before the war, the distance from miner's dwelling in Nottinghamshire to country house in Oxfordshire or stone cottage in Cornwall may have been greater than the distances between England and foreign lands. Lawrence has a good ear for different sorts of speech, as in the brittle upper-class conversation at Breadalby or the slangy demotic of the working-class couple in "A Chair"; the intellectual cut-and-thrust of the main couples or the backbiting remarks of Halliday and Pussum; or the cynical and sinister gaiety of Gerald, Gudrun, and Loerke. He also cultivates the eye, though he prefers touch and distrusts mentalistic images, showing his characters in motion: the slinking young man with his trousers sinking over his heels; the colorfully dressed sisters moving past the stares of working-class women or the leers of men and feeling like anthropologists among "aborigines"; the detestably correct French governess "perched on her high heels"; Gerald and the mare "sweating with violence." Because he was determined to plumb the depths of "being," Lawrence strove all the harder to objectify the invisible through realistic detail. As one critic has remarked, "by transcending realism, he becomes greater than the realists at their own method."[1]

Nevertheless, his stylistic ambitions were radical. To break down the "old stable ego" his syntax reflects the borderline of consciousness where feeling and thought form or dissolve and where the essential in human nature comes into being. In the foreword Lawrence likens the "slightly modified repetition" that distinguishes the novel's syntax to sexual intercourse: "every natural crisis in emotion or passion or understanding comes from this pulsing, frictional to-and-fro, which works up to culmination."[2] This sexualization of style, as one critic has called it, extends to narrative point of view.[3] The narrative voice in the novel, which cannot be simply identified as "Lawrence," displays the usual realist confidence in placing characters in time and space, moving the focus from one character to another, and varying dialogue with unspoken but conscious thought. The voice remains in the third person, as an omniscient narrator would in a Victorian novel, but it achieves the intimacy of a first-person narrator. Other novelists, of course, have achieved similar effects. Henry James uses the Flaubertian indirect free style to imitate the speech and thought of individual characters. James Joyce goes one step further by using a "stream of consciousness" style, in which the reader follows skeins of association and encounters the jumble of reflected and refracted reality in the minds of Stephen Dedalus or Leopold Bloom. Lawrence's innovation is to break down the barriers between speakers and even genders so as to rebuild character. He not only blurs the line between conscious and unconscious within individual characters, as does Joyce, but also shows consciousness dissolving and reuniting within and between characters in acts that are actually or metaphorically sexual.

Consider, for example, Gerald and Gudrun embracing for the

first time under the colliery bridge, from "And the colliers' sweethearts would, like herself, hang their heads back limp" to "They walked on towards the town" (415–17). We are placed in an industrial landscape that has been precisely re-created. The first half of the scene is given from Gudrun's point of view as she swoons in Gerald's embrace. Metaphors of physical change—*pour, melt, fluid, soft iron*—suggest the loss of self Gudrun feels: "So she was passed away and gone in him, and he was perfected." Recovering from the swoon, she wonders who he is until, noticing his "white aura," she realizes that he is not Gerald but "a visitor from the unseen." This is the epiphany. Almost at once, however, the northern god appears an "unutterable enemy" to be resisted as well as a desirable mate to be worshipped. She regains a firm self capable of controlling Gerald who, as the point of view broadens to include him, finds himself in the grip of a dominant female. In the dark her apprehension of him has been through touch:

> "You are so *beautiful*," she murmured in her throat.
> He wondered, and was suspended. But she felt him quiver and she came down involuntarily upon him. He could not help himself. Her fingers had him under their power. The fathomless, fathomless desire they could evoke in him was deeper than death, where he had no choice. (416)

Thus the reader gains access to a borderline region of consciousness. The scene is ritualized, mixing myth and realism. It occurs in an indefinite time and from a shifting point of view that crosses the boundaries of individual and gender. In sum, Lawrence imitates on the syntactic and semantic levels the theme of death and possible rebirth. The repetitive, overlapping clauses of his sentences reflect both the incremental advance of generational history and the rhythm of passion.

16

Three Couples

The narrative strategy of *Women in Love* departs radically from that of *The Rainbow*. Counterpointed scenes in contemporary time replace the chronological progress of three Brangwen generations across some sixty-five years. When rewriting Lawrence broke up thirteen sprawling chapters into thirty-one, making each self-contained yet dramatically linked. In *Women in Love* the comparative technique of *The Rainbow* has reached such a level of sophistication that every moment qualifies and is qualified by every other. The "mystic" marriage of Ursula Brangwen and Rupert Birkin develops in contrast to the tragic affair of her sister, Gudrun, and Gerald Crich. Interlaced with these stories is the troubled friendship of Gerald and Birkin, revealing aspects of the men's personalities that are suppressed in their relationships with women and exploring *Blutbrüderschaft* as a possible complement to heterosexual marriage.

URSULA BRANGWEN AND RUPERT BIRKIN

The story of Ursula and Rupert poses special problems of imaginative control. Rupert Birkin bears a striking resemblance in features, manner, and ideas to D. H. Lawrence. Although not an autobiographical novel like *Sons and Lovers, Women in Love* draws on incidents and people from Lawrence's life far more directly than does *The Rainbow*. Biographers have tracked down the origins of many details. The blow Hermione strikes to Birkin's head with a piece of lapis lazuli, for example, may have originated in the blow of a dinner plate administered by Frieda while Lawrence was washing the dishes. The characters in London Bohemia—Halliday, Pussum, and the Pompadour crowd—are recognizably satirical portraits. More questionably, the banned novelist living in exile was tempted in the early versions of the novel to use Birkin as a mouthpiece of misanthropy and propaganda. This desire to take revenge on the world that had burned *The Rainbow* was almost as strong as the desire to save the world from its folly. Both motives damaged early versions. *Sisters,* like the discarded "Prologue," gave free reign to Birkin, to his denunciations of the world and his utopian solutions. Though cut off from the reading public, however, Lawrence rose to the occasion. He rewrote the novel for what he called the "unseen witnesses," struggling heroically to temper Birkin's dogmatism and to trust the wisdom of the unfolding tale.

To keep Birkin within bounds Lawrence drew once again on the wisdom of the Brangwensaga. Just as he had put aside "Prologue" to start with "Sisters," so now he rewrote *Sisters* by making Ursula a less credulous, more critical partner who can both criticize Birkin's excesses and enhance his admirable qualities, thereby creating a "duality of feeling" in the reader's response. Thanks to Ursula's opposition we see the vital and sympathetic side of Birkin that otherwise might have been obscured by inflexibility and priggishness. Their relationship develops through a testing of ideas. Whenever Birkin mounts a soap box to give a sermon, Ursula interrupts with a derisive remark—"So cocksure!" or "Why drag in the stars?" Whenever Ursula relapses into stale ideas (for example, "love is freedom"), Birkin snaps back: "Sentimental cant." These modern lovers are well matched on many a "memorable battlefield"—"Mino," "Moony," and "Excurse." In these debates Birkin must clarify or discard utopian ideas. His speeches become expressions of character rather than authorially sanctioned truth. Although there is more of Lawrence in Birkin than in any other character, Birkin is never Lawrence's spokesperson. If his ideas on historical decline and the need for new relationships between men and women seem more cogent than those of others, they are nonetheless contested right to the end. Through the resilience of Ursula in debate, Lawrence fulfills his promise to show "woman becoming individual." Because of their energy, pertinacity, and purity of motive, Birkin and Ursula succeed in forging a relationship that can survive among the ruins of the modern world.

In "An Island," for example, Birkin rants about the hypocrisy and sadism of man. Sounding like Thoreau on Walden Pond, he imagines a world empty of people: "Do you think creation depends on *man*? It merely doesn't.—There are the trees and the grass and birds. I much prefer to think of the lark rising up in the morning upon a humanless world.—Man is a mistake, he must go" (188). But Ursula will not be convinced by mere rhetoric. She knows from past experience that the detestable human world of Beldover and Breadalby will not conveniently disappear: "It pleased Ursula, what he said . . . as a phantasy. . . . She herself knew too well the actuality of humanity. . . . It had a long way to go yet, a long hideous way." The bitter knowledge gained in *The Rainbow* at Brinsley Street School and Wiggiston supports her skepticism. Her opposition focuses criticism of Birkin on his manner of attacking humanity, thereby anticipating the reaction of many readers. She objects to the "Salvator Mundi touch," just as Halliday later ridicules Birkin's pompous letter about the "Flux of Corruption."

This critical attitude allows us to respond sympathetically to the odd blend in Birkin's personality of passion and dogmatism, self-knowledge and self-deceit. Although Birkin often deserves ridicule for his manner of proclaiming truths, he does have the vital instinct to search for an alternative to the deathliness of human relations. He has not retreated into cynicism like Gerald and Gudrun, the denizens of the Pompadour, or Loerke.

Readers of *The Rainbow* appreciate more fully the startling effect

Birkin has on this Brangwen heroine. The Ursula who fought to earn
a place in the so-called man's world has reached a low ebb. She fears
that there is "no beyond," that her life will remain unreplenished, a
"barren routine." Has the Brangwen journey been redirected toward
death, which now seems an "adventure" and "heritage" to be preferred
to a repetitious, mechanized life: "One might come to fruit in death"
(262)? Like Ursula, Birkin, whose affair with Hermione Roddice has
reached a stalemate, is attracted by thoughts of death. Love, marriage,
and children appear "repulsive" largely because sex makes one a "pris-
oner" and the reality of "community" has been reduced to hunting in
couples. Birkin's duties as inspector of schools, like the treatises on
education he wrote at Oxford in the "Prologue," seem futile. Divorced
from love, work no longer has the socially renewing impetus it had for
Will Brangwen, who, after revolutionizing his marriage in chapter 8
of *The Rainbow,* turned to public life as a handwork instructor. For
Birkin the satisfactions of denouncing all public systems and humanity
in general are wearing thin. As he admits after Ursula seduces him, "I
was becoming quite dead-alive, nothing but a word-bag" (256). He
needs Ursula as much as she needs him.

"Class-Room" and the Problem of Language   The interaction
among Birkin, Ursula, and Hermione in "Class-Room" illustrates the
"trembling instability of the balance" between not only Birkin and
Ursula but Birkin and Lawrence, the achievement of which Lawrence
called artistic "morality." Ursula is finishing a typical day of teaching
that has passed in a "trance." The arrival of Birkin on an unannounced
but official visit startles her fully awake. Her initial "subconscious
fear" may stem from Mr. Harby's inspections in *The Rainbow,* which
typify the hostility of the patriarchal world to women. But as Birkin
looks over the children's daily assignment, he seems to Ursula to be
moving in "another world." The scene recalls her grandfather Tom
Brangwen's first glimpse of Lydia Lensky, after which Tom walks "in
a far world."[1] Noticing the "tender light of dawn" in Ursula's face,
Birkin feels "gay." But Hermione's arrival returns them to the world

of clashing wills and failed love. Her disingenuous question about the usefulness of education provokes a violent outburst from Birkin. In the original version, Birkin fulminated against historical decline in words that came directly from Lawrence's nonfiction of the period, *The Crown* and *Twilight in Italy*. This blurring of the line between essay and fiction or author and character marked the less controlled *Sisters*. A brief excerpt gives the tone of the earlier version: "We are the last products of the decadent movement, the analytic, lyrical, emotional, scientific movement which has had full sway since the Renaissance. . . . Because the adventure of knowledge is not finished for us till we have got back to the very sources . . . in sensation, as one traces back a river. . . . this passion, this emotionalism, this soldiering, it is a form of immediate anthropology, we study the origins of man in our own immediate experience, we push right back to the first, and last, sensations of procreation and of death."[2] This harangue was unintelligible in dramatic terms, coming before the activities in Beldover, Breadalby, and London have prepared us to see the modern epoch as life-denying. So the disquisition on psychology was discarded in revision and replaced by a heated exchange on the misuse of "will," which the novel then dramatizes in the affairs of Birkin with Hermione and Gerald with Gudrun: "There's the whole difference in the world . . . between the actual sensual being, and the vicious mental-deliberate profligacy our lot goes in for. In our night-time, there's always the electricity switched on, we watch ourselves, we get it all in the head, really. You've got to lapse out before you can know what sensual reality is. . . . You've got to learn not-to-be, before you can come into being" (94). The speech now blends self-accusation with self-righteousness. By including himself in the condemnation of "our lot," Birkin appears less pompous and morbid, leaving open the possibility that if we lapse out we may be reborn.

The effect of this tirade on Ursula is remarkable. Birkin has unwittingly diagnosed one cause of her failure with Anton Skrebensky, her previous lover, who is committed to the status quo as opposed to the "unknown." Ursula willfully continues the affair with Anton long after recognizing their incompatibility. Such self-examination may explain the desire, otherwise strangely sudden or docile, to solve her problems in the light of Birkin's words, just as the memory of her conduct and Skrebensky's rejection may account for her weeping "whether from misery or joy."

In the first chapter Ursula thinks Birkin may have acknowledged a "using of the same language" but she is not sure. Though filled with talk, the novel is skeptical about linguistic communication, as opposed to touch or sex. All the main characters share Gerald's "passion" for debate. But language in this novel is usually beside the point, a medium through which one must pass to intuit a truth or reality that has been obscured by speech. Even as Birkin decries mental as opposed to physical knowledge, he hates his own stale metaphor of the "eternal apple." Language offers only a mirror to the self, turning Birkin as well as Hermione into a Lady of Shalott. In fact, language does not communicate ideas as much as it expresses the will to power. Hermione always wants to "lay hands" on her interlocutors, to "extract [their] secrets," and to bully her guests so as to confirm her control. Conversation at Breadalby is aggressive, "like a rattle of small artillery" (139). Gudrun, like Hermione, will not let a conversation proceed if it might reveal a weakness, as in the opening exchange with Ursula on the subject of marriage. Later Gerald treats the arguments of the foreigner Loerke with contempt and "sledge-hammer" assertions (547). Thus language preserves national as well as class divisions.

All the characters—and especially Birkin, the wordsmith of the novel—talk to themselves. Trapped in dead metaphors and false concepts, they are unable to act on their words and prone to self-pity. In "Water-Party" the narrator comments that "there was always confusion in speech," and immediately Birkin admits that all the talking about love and rebirth is a function of the failure to live: "One shouldn't talk when one is tired and wretched—One Hamletises, and it seems a lie.—Only believe me when I show you a bit of healthy pride and insouciance. I hate myself serious" (255). Indeed Birkin often delays in the manner of Hamlet, preferring soliloquy to showdown. Ursula must insist that he stop talking about love and live in the body. But even after their lovemaking, he relapses into willful intellectualism: "And he wanted to be with Ursula as free as with himself, single and clear and cool, yet balanced, polarised with her. The merging, the clutching, the mingling of love was become madly abhorrent to him" (270). To this and all the self-regarding talk of stars balanced in conjunction, Ursula delivers a scathing rebuttal in "Excurse": "You, and love! You may well say, you don't want love. No, you want *yourself,* and dirt, and death" (389). Like Hamlet, Birkin accuses himself of having unpacked his heart with words rather than deeds: "how was it he was always talking about sensual fulfilment?" (330). Although Birkin resents being regarded by Gerald and others as a brilliant talker whose words may be discounted, he is largely to blame. This excoriator of will and knowledge, the champion of "dark involuntary being," clings to his own fixed ideas.

To confuse Birkin with Lawrence, then, is as wrongminded as to claim that Lawrence lacks a sense of irony or humor. Critics who come to the defense of this or that character, Hermione or Loerke, with the argument that Lawrence is browbeating mere caricatures, have missed the point. Lawrence spares no character, least of all the figure in whom there is most of himself.

"Moony" The title will seem either curious or inevitable, depending on our familiarity with *The Rainbow.* This is the last in a series of moon scenes charting the struggles, advances, and setbacks of the Brangwens on their journey to a Promised Land of individual and social fulfilment. It occurs in a triplet of chapters, flanked by "Rabbit" and "Gladiatorial." In "Rabbit" Gudrun and Gerald conduct an obscene parody of the *Blutbrüderschaft* Birkin offers Gerald in "Man to Man." Subsequently, in "Gladiatorial," Birkin and Gerald enact that ideal of comradeship while wrestling naked. Between comes "Moony" with its partially successful reconciliation of the lovers and Birkin's placement of their relationship in the context of cultural decline.

The moon as a natural force no longer signals the replenishment of life as it does in the first generations of *The Rainbow*. Nor does it symbolize lovers' courting and marriage. Nor is it allied with female independence, as in "First Love" or "The Bitterness of Ecstasy," where Ursula defeats the masculine threat to her freedom in the person of Anton Skrebensky. Why has the moon become a presence to fear, shun, or destroy?

The scene by Willey Water is a stylistic tour de force, a dance of language in which the reader shares the experience of destruction and renewal symbolized by the moon's image on the lake. If the scene works, the reader shares Ursula's feeling of being "spilled out." The stoning of the moon's image allows us to visualize the energy released in passionate struggle, much as a Futurist painting does. Language itself becomes a battleground on which the "fight to the death between them—or to new life" (205) takes place.

The pastoral setting of the chapter, in which dogs bark, rabbits hop, and a sheep coughs, brings no release from feelings of estrangement: "That which the word 'human' stood for was despicable and repugnant to her" (320). Like Birkin at the end of "Breadalby," Ursula has retreated from society to the "magic peace" of the woods. Earlier, bloodied by Hermione's blow with a chunk of lapis lazuli, Birkin has renounced the "old ethic" of society and celebrated nature as his "marriage place" (166), just as Ursula renounces Skrebensky for the moon and downs in *The Rainbow*. The difference lies in Birkin's misanthropy. The younger Ursula had still hoped for social regeneration under the rainbow, whereas now she is desolate. Perhaps her reaction to the stoning—"spilled out" and "spent"—echoes Birkin's feeling of release; for she, like Birkin, seems to provoke the destructiveness of the partner. Indeed, Birkin's stoning could be seen as mythic wish fulfillment. Because Ursula "wished for something else out of the night," Birkin appears. Then, because she "wished it were perfectly dark," he stones the moon. Birkin's obsessive effort to obliterate the moon's image has been interpreted as an attack on female independence, either justified or sexist. The former interpretation points to Birkin's enigmatic remarks on woman as the Syria Dea or, earlier, "the awful, arrogant queen of life" (270). The latter emphasizes the unfairness of Birkin's charges against women and the futility of his enterprise; after all, the moon's image inevitably renews itself on the lake. Surely both these interpretations miss the mark. By jointly attacking the moon—Birkin actively and Ursula vicariously—the lovers purge fear, hate, and isolation through an activity that is also beautiful, that creates a "black and white kaleidoscope" in the act of destruction. The reader too takes part in the process of death and rebirth, of separation and renewal, that is central to the novel's vision and that Birkin generalizes when meditating on the African statue.

In the aftermath of the stoning, however, the lovers return to wrangling. Happy endings in Lawrence are never secure. Each accuses the other of willfulness, of clinging to a merely social identity. Ursula stings Birkin with a home truth: "It is you who can't let yourself go, it is you who hang on to yourself as if it were your only treasure . . . you preacher!" (328). Her accusation seems confirmed by Birkin's refusal to agree, as he had in "Mino" and "Water-Party," that love and sexual passion are enough. He wants "no passion now," and she leaves unsatisfied.

Meditating on the inconsistency between his rhetoric and his actions, Birkin remembers the African fetish statues in Halliday's flat. Evidently the inspiration seized Lawrence as suddenly as it does Birkin, for the description of the African and northern "ways" was inserted into the typescript on a handwritten page. Though the African statues fascinate Gerald in "Totem," he denies Birkin's contention that they are the art of an advanced culture. Then Gerald's warning to Birkin— "You like the wrong things . . . things against yourself"—seems defensive; and later, in "Continental," his expression comes to resemble a primitive mask. Birkin has admired the statues but has not drawn an explicit comparison between primitive and civilized cultures—until now.

The meditation has the logic of a dream that momentarily clarifies a mystery but raises more questions than it answers. It is one answer to the apocalyptic question often raised in the novel: "Is our day of

"Always! Do you?" she murmured, as he kissed her. And then, out of a full throat, she crooned "Kiss me! Kiss me!" And she cleaved close to him. He kissed her many times. But he too had his idea and his will. He wanted only gentle communion, no other, no passion now. — So that soon she drew away, put on her hat and went home.

The next day however, he felt wistful and yearning. He ~~thought he had been~~ *wrong, perhaps. Perhaps he had been wrong* ~~unnecessarily disagreeable. If he had in-~~ ~~to go to her with an idea of what he wanted.~~ *Was it really only an* ~~sisted only on his love, ignored the rest, all might have been~~ *idea, or was it the interpretation of a profound yearning? — If the* ~~well. It might.~~ *He did not quite convince himself. He believed* *the latter, how was it he was always talking about sensual fulfilment* ~~that she loved him. But he did not quite believe that she would~~ *The two did not agree very well.* ~~give him the surrender he wanted. Still, perhaps he was wrong~~ *Suddenly he found himself face to face with a situation. It was* ~~to insist. Perhaps he ought to win her with love. One should~~ *as simple as this: fatally simple. On the one hand, he knew he did* ~~not demand on these occasions. One should give love.~~ *want a further sensual experience — something deeper, darker than ordinary* ~~As the day wore on,~~ *a greater and greater yearning and tender* *life could give. He remembered the African fetishes he had seen at Halliday's* ~~ness came over him. He felt sorry for his ugly behaviour. She~~ *So often. There came back to him one, a statuette about two feet high, a* ~~really so sensitive, her skin was so delicate and even~~ *tall, slim, elegant figure from West Africa, in dark wood, glossy and* ~~fine. And he was so crude. He had been wrong. He was so very~~ *suave. It was a woman, with hair dressed high, like a melon shaped dome. He remembered* ~~for her too, with tenderness. She was so rare and so sensitive.~~ *her vividly: she was one of his soul's intimates. Her body was long and elegant, her* ~~He hid away from him the fact she was so obstinate. Her~~ *face was crushed tiny like a beetle, she had rows of* ~~round~~ *heavy collars, like a column* ~~somitable as she was rare and sensitive, he insisted only on the~~ *of quoits, on her neck. He remembered her: her astonishing cultured elegance,* ~~gentle qualities.~~ *diminished, beetle face, the astounding long elegant body, on short, ugly legs, with* ~~So he must go to her. In spite of his subconscious know-~~ *such protuberant buttocks, so weighty and unexpected below her slim long loins. He knew* ~~ledge that she was as unyielding and unchanged as ever, he said~~ *what he himself did not know. She had thousands of years of purely sensual, purely* ~~she was tender and hurt, she would be glad if he came to her with~~ *unspiritual knowledge behind her. It must have been thousands of years since her race* ~~love. So at last, towards evening, he must set out. He could~~ *had died, mystically: that is, since the relation between the senses and the outspoken* ~~not wait any longer. It was his nature to be too insistent and~~ *mind had broken, leaving the experience all in one sort, mystically sensual. Thousands of* ~~hasty for his own way.~~ *years ago, that which was eminent in himself must have taken place in these* ~~He drifted on swiftly to Beldover, half unconscious of his~~ *Africans: the goodness, the holiness, the desire for creation and productive happiness* ~~own movement. He saw the town on the slope of the hill, like~~ *must have lapsed, leaving the single impulse for knowledge in one sort, mindless* ~~Jerusalem to his fancy. The world was all strange and transcend-~~ *progressive knowledge through the senses, knowledge arrested and ending in the senses,* *mystic knowledge in disintegration and dissolution, knowledge such as the beetles* *have, which live purely within the world of corruption and cold dissolution. This was*

Rupert Birkin remembering the African fetishes. *Courtesy of the Harry Ransom Humanities Research Center, University of Texas at Austin* why her face looked like a beetle: this was why the Egyptians worshipped the ball-rolling scarab: because of the principle of knowledge in dissolution and corruption.

There is a long way we can travel, after the death-break: after that point where the soul in intense suffering breaks, ~~and~~ breaks away from its organic hold like a leaf that falls. We fall from the connection with life and hope, we lapse from pure ~~productivity~~ integral being, from creation and ~~liberty~~, and we fall into the long, long African process of purely sensual understanding, knowledge in the mystery of dissolution.

He realised now that this is a long process — thousands of years it takes, after the death of the creative spirit. He realised that there were great mysteries to be unsealed, sensual, mindless, dreadful mysteries, far beyond the phallic cult. How far, in their inverted culture, had these West Africans gone beyond phallic knowledge? Very, very far. Birkin recalled again the female figure: the elongated, long, long body, the curious, unexpected heavy buttocks, the long, ~~imprisoned~~ neck, the face with tiny features like a beetle's. This was far beyond any phallic knowledge, sensual subtle realities far beyond the scope of phallic investigation.

There remained this way, this awful African process, to be fulfilled. It would be done differently by the white races. The white races, having the arctic north behind them, the vast abstraction of ice and snow, would fulfil a mystery of ice-destructive knowledge, snow-abstract annihilation. Whereas the West Africans, controlled by the burning death-abstraction of the Sahara, had been fulfilled in sun-destruction, the ~~introspective~~ ~~complete~~ mystery of sun-rays.

Was this then all that remained? Was there left now nothing but to break off from the happy creative being, was the time up? Is our day of creative life finished? Does there remain to us only the strange, awful afterwards of the knowledge in dissolution, the African knowledge, but different in us, who are blond and blue-eyed from the north?

Birkin thought of Gerald. He was one of these strange white wonderful demons from the north, fulfilled in the destructive post mystery. And was he fated to pass away in this knowledge, this one process of frost-knowledge, death by perfect cold? Was he a messenger, an omen of the universal dissolution into whiteness and snow?

Birkin was frightened. He was tired too, when he had reached this length of speculation. Suddenly his strange, strained attention gave way, he could not attend to these mysteries any more. — There was another way, the way of freedom. There was the Paradisal entry into pure, single being, the individual soul taking precedence over love and desire for union, stronger than any ~~pangs~~ emotion, a lovely state of ~~free~~ proud singleness, which accepts the obligation of the permanent connection with others, and ~~with~~ the other, submits to the yoke and leash of love, but never forfeits its own proud individual singleness, even while it loves and yields.

~~This was the other way, the remaining way.~~ And he must turn to follow it. He thought of Ursula, how sensitive and delicate she really was, her skin so over-fine, as if one skin were wanting. She was really so marvellously gentle and sensitive. Why did he ever forget it? He must go to her at once. He must ask her to marry him. They must marry at once, and so make a definite pledge, enter into a definite communion. He must set out at once and ask her, this moment. There was no moment to waste.

creative life finished?" The hypothesis of cultural decline had been commonplace since the late nineteenth century and gained new currency during and after World War I and in such studies as Oswald Spengler's *Decline of the West* (1918–22) and Arnold Toynbee's *Study of History* (1934–61). Lawrence contributed his own version in a popular history text, *Movements in European History* (1921), which asserts that "The War . . . came in 1914, and smashed the growing tip of European civilisation," leaving us "directionless" except for the hope of a leader with *"natural Noblesse."*[3] The "inverted" culture symbolized by the African statue has undeniable attractions and dreadful satisfactions, as does the northern civilization symbolized by Gerald, master of mine and mountain. Both "ways," however, objectify the split between mind and body, love and work, sex and society, that Birkin has denounced and that now Ursula has forced him to acknowledge in himself. Birkin's dreamlike musings also bind together the imagery of the novel, linking Gerald's northern qualities to his affinities with the dark, "underworld" miners and Pussum. The worlds of industrial plutocrat, aristocrat, and bohemian suffer from the same dissociated sensibility that only the joint, productive work of man and woman can heal. So the daydream ends with a psychologically plausible though utopian assertion of escape in "the way of freedom." This hope of renewal carries some conviction because it follows the "re-assertion" of the moon's image in the preceding scene.

"Excurse" and the Limits of Language The imaginative problem Lawrence faced in "Excurse" was how to create a consummation for Birkin and Ursula that transcends the "old destructive" sexuality and yet seems to offer a redemptive hope for mankind. This climactic chapter must present the "way of freedom," envisaged by Birkin in "Moony," as different from the destructive affair of Gerald and Gudrun. Is the inner, psychic rhythm of death and rebirth dramatically convincing?

By driving deep into the countryside at the edge of Sherwood Forest, bringing along three rings as a gift, Birkin is resuming the quest for a "definite communion" with Ursula that has been deflected since "Moony." Though he claims to be driving "anywhere," he has promised to attend a farewell dinner for Hermione that evening at Breadalby. As Ursula indignantly points out, Birkin is a hypocrite, unwilling to make a clean break with the world he calls false and deathly. In contrast, she has grown in conviction since "Class-Room" and "Breadalby," where she detested but could not resist the bullying of Hermione and the ruling class. Now her attack on Birkin's hypocrisy accomplishes for him what his stoning of the moon had accomplished for her: "There was a darkness over his mind. The terrible knot of consciousness that had persisted there like an obsession was broken, gone, his life was dissolved in darkness over his limbs and his body" (391). "Dissolved" is a near synonym for "spilled out." Birkin's identity has dissolved as had Ursula's by the lake. So it is Birkin's turn to have his wish fulfilled as in a myth: "He wanted her to come back. . . . She was coming back."

This mythic reconciliation sets the stage for their pledge of love in the tearoom at the Saracen's Head. Ursula feels that she is reentering the dream world of her childhood; so it is symbolically apt that she should recall the resonant imagery of the Book of Genesis, which she had loved as an adolescent and young woman in *The Rainbow*. Birkin appears to her "metamorphosed" into one of the sons of God, though not because Lawrence was sexist in insisting on Ursula's subservience to the godlike man. Ursula has searched for, found, and in large measure created her son of God; as a result, she can take her tea, resign her job, and plan with Birkin a new life of "perfected relation" (398).

Sherwood Forest, the legendary haunt of Robin Hood, which forms a borderline between nature and the encroaching industrial landscape, is the perfect site for these modern exiles. Their night of passion, renovating and utopian, cannot be described in the language of Beldover and Breadalby. Instead, we read the paradoxical language of touch, which cannot be seen or known. Like the poetry of mystic passion in, for example, St. John of the Cross, the passion of Birkin and Ursula is evoked through negatives—"ineffable," "inhuman," and "unrevealed." That it is a "palpable" experience must be taken on faith. Language can do no more.

GERALD CRICH AND RUPERT BIRKIN

The homoerotic aspect of *Women in Love* has stirred controversy ever since the English publisher, Martin Secker, silently excised several paragraphs in 1921. Since the discovery of the "Prologue" in 1963 Lawrence's achievement has been subjected to allegations of duplicity or confusion in the treatment of homoerotic feeling. Many critics have found the published novel to be more reticent on the subject of homosexuality than the "Prologue" implies the earlier version would have been, had it been completed. Others, judging Birkin to be unclear on what he offers Gerald or expects from him, conclude that Lawrence himself must have been confused.

Citing the fate of *The Rainbow,* almost all critics have assumed that one motive for treating homoerotic feeling less explicitly in the novel than in the "Prologue" was Lawrence's fear of adverse public opinion. There is, however, no evidence for this hypothesis. For the English edition Lawrence was forced to make a few cosmetic changes to avoid a libel suit—clothing the naked men of "Totem" in "white pyjamas" and avoiding explicit mention of the homosexual love between Loerke and Leitner.[4] But he had written and revised several drafts of the novel years earlier, when he had little hope of finding a publisher.

Some critics find the novel more reticent than the "Prologue" on the basis of a venerable, not to say hoary, Freudian interpretation of *Sons and Lovers:* "Lacking an acceptable father-figure, dominated by an aggressive mother, married to an aggressive wife, deeply inhibited in his earliest sexual relations, frail of body—it is not surprising that there should have been a strong homosexual element in Lawrence's make-up."[5] The critical practice here is misleading. The allegedly biographical details have been extracted from the novel, where they were transmuted; so fiction is being used to confirm biography. According to this interpretation, Lawrence not only distorted the presentation of his father and Jessie to justify his mother in *Sons and Lovers* but remained in oedipal bondage, incapable of mature heterosexual love and ashamed of his homosexual desires. As John Middleton Murry argued in *Son of Woman,* the story of Birkin and Gerald reveals Lawrence's need "to escape to a man from the misery of his own failure with a woman."[6] Another critic speculates that Lawrence wanted to write in praise of homosexuality, which he saw as a "higher" form of love than heterosexuality, but lacked the courage to treat "this intensely personal theme" with candor.[7]

Yet the evidence of Lawrence's artistic intentions in the manuscript drafts and in the published novel does not support these charges of duplicity or repression. On the contrary, the manuscripts and novel reveal that Lawrence rewrote the friendship of Gerald and Birkin so as to express the ideal of male comradeship as a possible solution to the deathliness of modern love, an additional though not higher relationship that might complement a new type of "mystic" heterosexual marriage.

Prelude to Intimacy: "In the Train," "Breadalby," and "Water-Party"

Unlike the "Prologue" or *Sisters* (the first full-length draft), the novel we now read develops the mutual need and affection of the two men indirectly, through casual conversations. "In the Train" begins the process. In *Sisters* Birkin delivered Gerald an overbearing lecture on the "new life" that a creative love between man and woman would make possible. Birkin was adamant that heterosexual love, a bonding with one woman, would bring personal and social regeneration—or nothing would. But his stridency appeared defensive, the result of a blindness to his need for male love. He suppressed any such knowledge together with any sign of affection for Gerald; not surprisingly, Gerald listened in silent hostility to the exclusive alternatives—either heterosexual marriage or despair and death:

"It isn't children I want to bring forth with a woman, but hope and truth and a new understanding," [said Birkin].

"And it needs you and a woman?" asked Gerald.

"It can only be born of the love between a man and a woman—the living spirit, the new understanding. . . . But we are all barren, as men. We can only beget children, and suffer death. . . ."

"I can't help thinking that is rather narrow, limited, what you say," [said Gerald].[8]

In the final version Birkin still believes in heterosexual love as the primary relationship, but he does not insist that men are "barren." Now his mood passes from anger at Gerald's disbelief, through self-doubt, to "rich affectionateness and laughter." Although neither man voices his need for the other, their conversation implies that male friendship might occupy a middle ground between Birkin's insistence on heterosexual marriage and Gerald's skepticism about any lasting relationship. This dialogue, which replaces Birkin's monologue in *Sisters,* reveals Gerald's failure to find an individual purpose beyond the perfecting of a social mechanism and, in turn, Birkin's response to Gerald's tacit plea for advice and companionship. The new conception has the advantage of holding Gerald's underlying insecurity in balance with his manly exterior:

"And you mean if there isn't the woman, there's nothing?" said Gerald.

"Pretty well that—seeing there's no God."

"Then we're hard put to it," said Gerald. . . .

Birkin could not help seeing how beautiful and soldierly his face was, with a certain courage to be indifferent. (110)

The limitations of this brand of courage will become plain later when Gerald has the courage to experience the deathliness of modern love but not to envisage an alternative in the love of man for man. The revision also controls the reader's response to Birkin, who sounds to Gerald "insistent rather than confident." Birkin must confess his own perplexity together with his affection for Gerald as a person, no matter how unwilling a convert. He has become a troubled searcher for the truth rather than an inflexible prophet; his humanity as well as Gerald's has been deepened. Henceforth the ambivalence of their friendship is accentuated.

In the *Sisters* version of the Breadalby houseparty, for instance, Gerald merely suffered from a bad conscience because he had not paid Pussum after their brief affair. In *Women in Love* this trivial decision becomes a symptom of Gerald's perplexity about what to do with his life and of his skepticism about finding a new direction through friendship with either sex. Although Gerald accedes to Birkin's analysis that he is "all in bits," oscillating between random affairs and the unfulfilling business of the mines, with no "centre" or "single pure activity," he derides Birkin's suggestion of marriage with an Edwardian, man-of-the-world complacency: "No, no, no, my boy." The movement is typical of the conflict within Gerald between naiveté and cynicism, strength and vulnerability.

Declaration of Friendship: "Man to Man" The chapter "Man to Man" represents the first climax of the theme of male friendship in *Women in Love*. The strong affection between Gerald and Birkin, previously repressed, is openly acknowledged for the first time.

As the chapter opened in *Sisters,* however, Birkin's situation recalled the "Prologue." His desire for a male friend was wholly conscious and coupled with a failure to form a stable, loving relationship with a woman, either Hermione or Ursula. He lay in sickbed thinking of his affair with Ursula, which had reached an impasse. Humiliated by the thought of being loved in equality by a woman, he had been demanding of Ursula an absolute surrender like that of Mohammed's wives. For her part, Ursula was equally absolute in asserting a female superiority (though readers were given only Birkin's word for this). If Birkin appeared a male chauvinist, Ursula resembled, at least to Birkin, the overweening female or *magna mater* who had unmanned Anton Skrebensky beneath the moon in *The Rainbow*. Recoiling from this impasse, Birkin turned to his love for Gerald as a despairing consolation. He had no hope in the revivifying possibilities of male friendship; without woman there could be no new life. He had placed himself in a false position, split between dogmatic claims on Ursula and a love for Gerald that was impossible because it was largely a reaction to the failure with Ursula: "Gerald and he had a curious love for each other. It was a love that was perhaps death, a love which was complemented by the hatred for woman. . . . So be it. No man can create life by himself. It needs a man and a woman. And if the woman refuse, then the life is uncreated, and death triumphs. Il Trionfo Della Morte."[9] That reference to the title of a melodramatic novel by Gabriele D'Annunzio betrays the false note: Birkin was indulging in self-pity. Indeed, Birkin's posturing recalls the situation in "Prologue" where his unadmitted love for men was linked to a general failure in human relations. Since Birkin did not believe that either female or male friendship offered an alternative to the imminent experience of death, he responded to Gerald's passionate approach with only "cold weariness":

> "Yes," [Birkin] admitted, "I like you more than anybody else—any other *man.*"
>
> He put out his hand from the bed, and took Gerald's brown, sinewy hand in his own. Convulsively, Gerald clasped Birkin's hand in both his. . . . He wanted the other man to put his arms round him, and hold him. . . . Yet it was so impossible.
>
> "A Blutbrüderschaft," said Birkin, wearily, reassuring, as if to comfort the other.[10]

That was the sole use of the German term in *Sisters.* Birkin's offer carried no conviction, however, because neither he nor Gerald showed the courage to question conventional male roles.

While rewriting the chapter for *Women in Love,* Lawrence explored the vital potential in what had appeared the impossible love of man for man. He amplified the solitary suggestion of *Blutbrüderschaft* into the main theme of the friends' conversation. Now Birkin sees the need for a creative love between men. He looks at Gerald "with clear,

331.   330a

and wondered,

He lay in the bed, whilst his friend sat beside him, lost
in ~~wonder~~ *brooding*. Each man was ~~lost~~ *gone* in his own thoughts.

"You know how the old German knights used to swear a
Blutbrüderschaft," he said to Gerald, with quite a new happy
activity in his eyes.

"Make a little wound in their arms, and rub ~~the~~ each other's
blood into the ~~two~~ cut?", said Gerald.

"Yes - and swear to be true to each other, of one blood, all their
lives. — That is what we ought to do. No wounds, that is obsolete. — But
we ought to swear to love each other, you and I, implicitly and
perfectly, finally, without any possibility of going back on it."

He looked at Gerald with clear, happy eyes of discovery. Gerald
looked down at him, attracted, so deeply bondaged in fascinated
attraction, *that means* ~~but~~, mistrustful, resenting the bondage, *hating the*
attraction.

"We will swear to each other, one day, shall we?" pleaded
Birkin. "We will swear to stand by each other — be true to each
other — ultimately — infallibly — given to each other, organically, — without
possibility of taking back."

Birkin sought hard to express himself. But Gerald hardly listened.
His face shone with a certain luminous pleasure. He was pleased. But
he kept his reserve. He held himself back.

"Shall we swear to each other, one day?", said Birkin,
putting out his hand towards Gerald.

Gerald just touched the extended fine, living hand, as if *withheld and* afraid.
"We'll leave it till I understand it better," he said, in a
voice of *excuse*.

Birkin watched him. A little sharp disappointment, perhaps a
touch of contempt came into his heart.

"Yes," he said, "you must tell me what you think, later. You
know what I mean? not sloppy emotionalism. An impersonal union ~~that~~ leaves one free."
— They lapsed both into silence. Birkin was looking at Gerald all
the time. He seemed now to see, not the physical, animal man, which
he usually saw in Gerald, and which usually he liked so much, but
the man himself, complete, and as if fated, doomed, limited. This

Rupert Birkin describes *Blutbrüderschaft* to Gerald Crich. *Courtesy of the
Harry Ransom Humanities Research Center, University of Texas at Austin*

103

happy eyes of discovery," but he must search for the right words to express the love he has been denying all along: "We will swear to stand by each other—be true to each other—ultimately—infallibly—given to each other, organically—without possibility of taking back" (278). The urgency and sincerity of his words are now more important than their programmatic content. Birkin has seized on the German conception so as to appeal to his "soldierly" friend who considers him "uncertain" in the man's world. Far from being Birkin's willful imposition, as has been alleged, *Blutbrüderschaft* is a concession to Gerald's more reserved personality.[11] It suggests the sort of relationship that might find an acceptable social expression for the love that hitherto had dared not speak its name.[12] The artistic focus is on the differing reactions of the friends to the notion of *Blutbrüderschaft*. While Birkin lectures eagerly, Gerald, though attracted, holds himself in reserve: "Gerald looked down at him, attracted, so deeply bondaged in fascinated attraction, that he was mistrustful, resenting the bondage, hating the attraction. . . . Gerald hardly listened. His face shone with a certain luminous pleasure. He was pleased. But he kept his reserve. He held himself back" (278). The ambivalence of Gerald's response, his desire and reserve, will come to seem a sign of his fatality.

Thus the rewritten "Man to Man," in which the friends admit male love to be a personal issue, marked a crucial advance in Lawrence's exploration of the text. Whereas "Prologue" and *Sisters* presented a conscious but hopeless desire for men, which was merely the obverse of a failure with women, *Women in Love* suggests that male friendship might complement a revitalized relationship with women. Joyce Carol Oates has made an interesting case for the sympathetic portrayal of homoerotic "yearning" in "Prologue," arguing that Birkin's "half-serious desire to rid himself of his soul in order to escape his predicament, and his fear of madness and dissolution as a consequence of his lovelessness give him a tragic death comparable to Hamlet's."[13] Although Oates mistakenly thinks Lawrence suppressed the "Prologue," she points out correctly that it was Birkin's tragedy rather than Gerald's and that the intimacy achieved by the friends during their skiing holiday was "consciously rejected" when they resumed their ordinary lives. *Women in Love* presents an unacknowledged love that Birkin comes to espouse but that Gerald cannot fully accept even though he is flattered and stimulated by it.

Of course, to speak of homoerotic desire is one thing; to act on the belief or impulse, quite another. One critic has accused Lawrence of telling but not showing that Gerald is attracted by Birkin and the offer of *Blutbrüderschaft*.[14] But surely both Gerald's affection and his physical need are shown long before the wrestling scene in "Gladiatorial." In "Breadalby," for example, Gerald wanders in his shirt into Birkin's room and sits on the bed, quite unself-consciously, to ask Birkin's advice about Pussum. Gerald's "white-skinned, full, muscular legs," which have been previously admired by Gudrun as they controlled the mare, stir in Birkin a feeling of "pathos . . . as if they were childish." That image prepares the reader for the perplexity in Gerald's question: "I wish you'd tell me something that *did* matter" (153). Later, in "Water-Party," Gerald grips Birkin's shoulder but declines to come away from the futile search for the drowned. Such moments of touch or appreciation lend plausibility to the exchange in "Man to Man," where Birkin suggests *Blutbrüderschaft* but Gerald, though "deeply bondaged in fascinated attraction," demurs by lightly touching Birkin's hand, "as if withheld and afraid" (278).

"Gladiatorial" and "Marriage or Not": Achievement or Failure?

The wrestling scene in "Gladiatorial" is a tour de force of rapturous writing through which we see the friends express physically their emotional bond, freed from the distortions of spoken language. This language of touch resembles that which Birkin and Ursula will later use during their consummation in "Excurse," when, as Ursula says, "To speak, to see, was nothing" (402). It is a central paradox of the novel that "there was always confusion in speech," that language comes freighted with the conventional wisdom that stifles "new movement" in human relations. Thus Birkin arrives at Shortlands in retreat from the fiasco of his proposal to Ursula in "Moony." Gerald teases

Birkin for having come to "wrestle with his good angel" but welcomes relief from inactivity. He cannot put into words his feelings of emptiness except in platitudes about work and love being the cure for ennui, though in his life he advocates a split between public work and private love. Birkin and Gerald temporarily go beyond these contradictions in the wrestling, which leaves "an unfinished meaning" (351).

The naked wrestling of the two friends, which is vividly re-created in the film version by Ken Russell, is at once a "real set-to" and a homoerotic embrace. In the latter sense it has excited controversy. Was Lawrence trying to describe a homosexual experience comparable in intensity to the experiences of the heterosexual couples?[15] The comparative sequence of "Excurse," "Death and Love," and "Marriage or Not" yields two, not three, sexual consummations, though as we shall see, the men's conversation was rewritten to confront the subject of the "unadmitted love of man for man." If the wrestling is a sort of sublimated homosexuality, is that a sign that Lawrence's true subject, as in "Prologue," is or should have been male love? The manuscripts supply interesting but equivocal evidence of Lawrence's intentions. For example, he heightened the sexual import of the wrestling: "It was as if Birkin's whole physical intelligence [flickered over] <interpenetrated into> Gerald's body, as if his fine, sublimated energy [penetrated] <entered> into the flesh of the [heavier] <fuller> man, like some [spell] <potency>."[16] After such a description, it is understandable that some critics have judged Gerald's question, "Is this the Brüderschaft you wanted?" to be a tacit acknowledgment that the wrestling has been a homosexual embrace. Nevertheless, the rhythm of the subsequent action suggests that, as in the depiction of heterosexual lovemaking, Lawrence was less interested in anatomy than in the range of sensual and emotional response. Following the brief handclasp that has different meanings—"sudden and momentaneous" for Gerald and "strong" for Birkin—the friends quickly diverge in thought and action. Gerald recovers quickly, ordering food and drink and donning a silk caftan, whereas Birkin, feeling Gerald "lapsing out of him," turns in thought to Ursula. Then the chapter ends in conversation about marriage, which reveals Gerald's yearning for a fulfilling personal relationship but his skepticism about heterosexual marriage and his reserve about *Blutbrüderschaft:*

> "Is this the Brüderschaft you wanted?"
> "Perhaps. Do you think this pledges anything?"
> "I don't know," laughed Gerald. (352)

The unfinished meaning of their wrestling is confronted for the last time in "Marriage or Not." Their conversation about comradeship comes directly after the climaxes of heterosexual love in "Excurse" and "Death and Love" and before Gerald is swept away from Birkin into the tragic destructiveness of the closing Tyrolese chapters. Far from disguising homoerotic implications while rewriting, Lawrence was clarifying and extending them.

In *Sisters* the opening witticisms about Gerald's possible marriage to Gudrun led into a strident "dissertation" by Birkin. Male comradeship was never mentioned, in keeping with the reticence of early versions. Instead, Birkin lectured Gerald on how the knowledge of death gives one confidence to ignore the falsity of life and to start building a new world around the nucleus of a "living" marriage. It was a stump speech that antagonized Gerald, who felt "as if he were being forced in some direction," and that was dramatically unconvincing on several counts. In *Sisters* Birkin never achieved such a marriage with Ursula and considered his love for Gerald to be "impossible." He was not a credible spokesman for marriage of any sort.

In *Women in Love,* by contrast, what had been merely jocular repartee gives way to a tormented though unspoken plea for love by Gerald:

> "Yes . . . marriage is one direction—"
> "And what is the other?" asked Birkin quickly.
> Gerald looked up at him with hot, strangely-conscious eyes, that the other man could not understand.
> "I can't say," he replied. "If I knew *that*—". . . .

"You mean if you knew the alternative?" asked Birkin. "And
since you don't know it, marriage is a *pis aller*.". . .
    "One does have the feeling that marriage is a *pis aller*," he
admitted. (438–39)

Then Birkin, as though staking his all on a last throw, speaks frankly
of the "additional" homosexual marriage that would be "equally important, equally creative." No longer relying on the analogy of the
German pledging ceremony, he articulates the hitherto unadmitted
content of male comradeship. At least that seems to be his meaning,
though again critics dispute the matter and, for publication in England,
Martin Secker silently excised the possibly offensive paragraphs:

> "Surely there can never be anything as strong between man and
> man as sex love is between man and woman. Nature doesn't provide
> the basis."
>   "Well, of course, I think she does. And I don't think we shall
> ever be happy till we establish ourselves on this basis. You've got
> to get rid of the *exclusiveness* of married love. And you've got to
> admit the unadmitted love of man for man. It makes for a greater
> freedom for everybody, a greater power of individuality both in
> men and women."
>   "I know," said Gerald, "you believe something like that. Only
> I can't *feel* it, you see." (440)

As Phaedra in Euripides' *Hippolytus* says, most people know what is
right but cannot bring themselves to do it. Gerald's explanation that
he doesn't "feel" this truth is the consequence of cowardice or an
absence of will to act on his feelings for Birkin. The achieved drama of
the novel supports Birkin's assertion that Gerald needs an "additional"
love. All the moments when he turns to Birkin for advice or companionship reveal the conflict between his worldliness and his hope for a way
out of the impasse of his public and private lives. Although these
moments of emotional honesty may seem doomed in retrospect, they
complicate the reader's anticipation of Gerald's destiny. Not until his

last words does he appear to be "hardly responsible" and to have sealed his fate:

> "I've loved you, as well as Gudrun, don't forget," said Birkin bitterly. . . .
> "Have you?" he said, with icy scepticism. "Or do you think you have?" (536)

No doubt Birkin's rhetoric in such phrases as "perfect relationship" or "sheer intimacy" or "eternal union" is somewhat vague; and Ursula repeatedly challenges him to clarify what he means. He is, after all, imagining sorts of relationships that do not yet exist. Yet to charge that Birkin and Lawrence are "quite unclear" about what the relationship is to become, as one critic has, is to mistake the very nature of exploratory fiction.[17] Birkin's logic, whereby a pledging between men will lead to a pledging with a woman in "absolute, mystic marriage" (440), is inevitably abridged and incapable of demonstration within the book. Its utopian intention, however, is quite clear. *Blutbrüderschaft* may inaugurate social relationships, thereby offering a supplement to the sort of marriage that has become, in a description as relevant today as then, "tight, mean . . . [a] tacit hunting in couples."

However speculative the connection between homoerotic feeling and heterosexual marriage may appear, the friendship of Birkin and Gerald is a great dramatic achievement. By revealing the vulnerable, inquiring sides of Gerald's nature that are suppressed in his affair with Gudrun, Lawrence endows him with a humanity quite absent from Anton Skrebensky or later "deniers" of life like Rico in *St. Mawr* and Clifford Chatterley. The drama of Gerald's life and death achieves the dimensions of Greek or Shakespearian tragedy. He goes to his death in the company of Agamemnon, Macbeth, and Othello.

GERALD CRICH AND GUDRUN BRANGWEN

In the manuscripts we can observe Lawrence seizing his dramatic opportunities. The light revision of *Sisters* becomes heavy in the final

Tyrolese chapters, as though Lawrence were seeing at last the full possibilities of his materials. Having created the icy setting in the mountains for the climax, he was inspired to add those aspects of character and theme that would lead inevitably to the tragic death of Gerald amid the "terrible waste of whiteness." In structural terms the skiing holiday in the Alps from "Prologue" was moved to the end but foreshadowed throughout in northern imagery. As a result the concluding scenes have a cumulative power unmatched in Lawrence's fiction.

The nonhuman aspect of the "terrible, static ice-built mountain-top" (530) suggested a complex of imagery in which to describe the powerful and ultimately self-destructive will that Gerald and Gudrun exert on each other and the world at large. Just as the dazzling white of the mountains reduces humans to "phenomena" and "snow-creatures," so Gerald treats his miners as "instruments . . . sporadic little unimportant phenomena," subduing man and beast with an apparently indomitable northern willpower. Having transformed the "hunter . . . traveller . . . soldier" of "Prologue" into an industrial magnate, Lawrence could make him the symbol of the winter of our epoch: "He felt strong as [a weapon] <winter>."[18]

The resonance of this vocabulary for conveying the sterile abuse of the will, which is characteristic of modern society, struck Lawrence with such force that he rewrote scene after scene to accentuate it. Virtually all the allusions to Gerald's northern presence are the result of revision. At her first sight of Gerald, for example, Gudrun sees through to the tragic climax of their affair:

["*His* totem is the wolf," said Gudrun to herself, "a young, inno-cent, unconscious wolf." She wondered *how* innocent, and how far untameable. She would like to know. He looked a man of twenty-eight or thirty, but young, unbroached.]

<Gudrun lighted on him at once. There was something northern about him that magnetised her. In his clear northern flesh and his fair hair was a glisten like cold sunshine refracted through crystals

transparent skin, she leaned forward rather, her features were
strongly marked, handsome, with a tense, unseeing, predative
look. Her colourless hair was untidy, wisps floating down
on to her sac coat of dark blue silk, from under her blue silk
hat. She looked like a woman with a monomania, furtive almost,
but heavily proud.

Her son was of a fair, sun-tanned type, rather above
middle height, well-made, and ~~noticeably~~ *almost exaggeratedly* well-dressed. But
about him also was the strange, guarded look, the unconscious
~~reserve~~ *glisten,* as if he did not belong to the same ~~idea~~ *creation* as the people
about him. ~~"His totem is the wolf," said Gudrun to herself,~~
Gudrun lighted on him at once. There was something northern about him
~~"a young, innocent, unconscious wolf." She wondered how~~
that magnetised her. In his clear northern flesh and his fair hair was a glisten
~~innocent, and how far untameable. She would, like to know.~~
like ~~full gold~~ *sunshine refracted through crystals of ice, and he looked*
~~He looked a man of twenty-eight or thirty, but young, unbroached.~~
so new, unbroached, pure as an arctic thing. Perhaps he was thirty years old,
~~His gleaming handsomeness, maleness, like a young, good-~~
perhaps more. His gleaming beauty, maleness, like a young, good-
~~humoured wolf, did not blind her to the significant stillness~~
humoured, smiling wolf did not blind her to the significant, sinister stillness
in his bearing, the lurking danger of his ~~cunning, indomitable~~ *unsubdued*
temper. "His totem is the wolf," she repeated to herself.

"His mother is an old, unbroken wolf." And then she experienced
a keen paroxysm, a transport, as if she had made some incredible
discovery, known to nobody else on earth. A strange transport
took possession of her, all her veins were in a paroxysm of
violent sensation. "Good God!" she exclaimed to herself,
"~~this is a queer go!~~ *What is this?*" And then, a moment after, she was

Gerald Crich's "northern" appearance. *Courtesy of the Harry Ransom*
Humanities Research Center, University of Texas at Austin

of ice. And he looked so new, unbroached, pure as an arctic thing.>[19]

The way this northern vocabulary harmonizes with the mechanical and life-denying nature of the will is clear in scenes where Gerald subdues the Arab mare ("Coal-Dust") and Bismarck ("Rabbit"):

> Both man and horse were sweating with violence. <Yet he seemed calm as a ray of cold sunshine.>

> Then a sudden [deep, congenital anger] <sharp, white-edged wrath> came up in him. . . . He looked at her [in wonder, and subterranean fear] <and the whitish, electric gleam in his face intensified>.[20]

"Diver" "Diver" is the first in a sequence of counterpointed scenes dramatizing the growth of the attraction between Gerald and Gudrun against a background of the natural world. Though the novel contains a myth of nature's gradual debilitation by industry, there are wondrous evocations of the "new creation" that is always possible, as here by Willey Water. The Brangwen sisters, walking on a wet autumn morning, come upon Gerald swimming naked. As subsequently in "Coal-Dust," they see Gerald's actions in different perspectives. Gudrun envies him strongly for his freedom as a man, not merely to swim naked but to accomplish any number of things without the hindrance of "the *thousand* obstacles a woman has in front of her" (98). Ursula, though sympathetic, is puzzled by the excessive emotion in Gudrun's explanation, as she had been baffled by Gudrun's hostility to childbearing and home in "Sisters." Both sisters note Gerald's movements like pure physical processes—"sharp," "invading," "violent"—and his exultation in the isolation of another, nonhuman world: "He was happy, thrusting with his legs and all his body, without bond or connection anywhere, just himself of the water world" (97). Gerald, in turn, enjoys the attention of the sisters. From the perspective of "Water-Party" his commanding motion will prove to have been ironically overconfident, a mark of hubris in a tragic hero. There his reflections on the Crich family failing to "put a thing right, once it has gone wrong," made after vainly diving for his sister, foreshadow the end of isolation: "If you once die . . . then when it's over, it's finished. Why come to life again? There's room under that water there for thousands" (251). Finally Gerald becomes truly "of" the watery world, frozen to death high in the Alps: "He was isolated as if there were a vacuum round his heart, or a sheath of pure ice" (560).

A first reading, of course, does not reveal these imaginative cross-references, as Lawrence explained in a letter to Catherine Carswell: "About the Gerald-Work part: I want it to come where it does: you meet a man, you get an impression of him, you find out *afterwards* what he has done."[21] The novel is structured so that the destructive potential in Gerald's world is only intimated until "Breadalby," when the latent murderousness of society is revealed in Hermione's attack on Birkin. Similarly, Gerald seems enviable in "Diver," though Ursula's story of the accidental killing of his brother in childhood may already have given a premonition of something ominous in his character. Does playing at killing reveal "some primitive *desire* for killing," as Ursula believes? This is, in fact, the second mention of Gerald's boyhood accident. Earlier in "Shortlands" the conversation of Birkin and Mrs. Crich was revised to emphasize this chink in Gerald's armor: "'Gerald!" she exclaimed. "He's [a rebel, that one, a real rebel] <the most missing of them all>."[22] And "Shortlands" ends with a conversation in which Birkin argues provocatively that Gerald's belief in law and order is a projection of his "lurking desire" to cut someone's throat or have his own "gizzard slit." Although Gerald may express the sentiments of the reader when he replies "Sometimes you talk pure nonsense," the apparently ridiculous assertion acquires ominous force in retrospect, as Gerald and Gudrun alternate in the roles of victim and victimizer.

"Coal Dust" and "The Industrial Magnate" When Gerald next presents a spectacle to the sisters, he is forcing a terrified red

Arab mare to stand at a railroad crossing. The horse's color may be suggestive, as red horses are contrasted with machinery and industrial landscapes in several Futurist paintings.[23] In any case, the revelation of latent violence in "Breadalby" (when Hermione as "priestess" of an entire society tries to kill Birkin) has intervened, so that Gerald's brutality casts a sinister light on the willpower displayed in "Diver." Once again Gerald's actions have a secret meaning to Gudrun, though she may not admit it to herself, much less share it with Ursula, for whom the scene is merely repulsive. When Gudrun leaps forward to throw open the gate, shouting, "I should think you're proud," she may be returning the challenge while praising the horseman, intimating that she will not be as easily subdued as the mare. But her numbing apprehension of "blood-subordination," with its sexual overtones, does give Gerald the temporary victory—a fact that may explain her provoking conduct before the bullocks later in "Water-Party," when she strikes Gerald for trying to protect her.

Immediately after this encounter the sisters walk through the "amorphous squalor" of Gerald's industrial empire, Beldover. For Gudrun the miners exercise a potent fascination that contrasts with her haughty reserve before working-class women in "Sisters." Lawrence created a myth of industry rather than a realistic portrait of the workers. It is a modern myth in which Gerald plays a centaur and deus ex machina while Gudrun, lured by the "siren's song" in the miners' voices, feels "like a new Daphne, turning not into a tree but a machine" (174). Several critics have pointed out that Lawrence's historical scheme reworks "social and historical forces . . . into forms of life and death"[24] and that, as one result, it seriously distorts the "state of mind" of working people under capitalism, particularly by reducing the workingman's fight for equality to either mere cupidity or a desire for "chaos."[25] The criticism is two-pronged. First, it is alleged, Lawrence misrepresents the aspirations and "texture of ordinary life" among the workers. Second, having chronicled the disappearance of his childhood community in *The Rainbow*, "he could not conceive of there being anything else properly called 'community' to take its place."[26] So the first failure is seen as a result of the second. Both criticisms seek to counter Leavis's celebrated praise of Lawrence for presenting "a vivid glimpse of the consequences for the lives of the miners" of industrialism.[27] Here the manuscripts reveal a significant change in direction.

It seems that Lawrence rewrote to suggest that the consequences of which Leavis speaks are actually an outcome of a deficiency in the miners' natures. Whereas *Sisters* gave the vigorous life that had been perverted by industrialism, *Women in Love* evokes powerful but destructive life, with few redeeming qualities. The "potent darkness" of the atmosphere of Beldover that appeals to Gudrun becomes "mindless, inhuman," a "voluptuousness . . . like that of machinery."[28] As a result there is little difference between the miners as human beings and as creatures of the industrial machine; they are as "unnatural" as the machines they operate: "They moved with their strange, [absolved] <distorted> dignity. . . . Their voices were full of an intolerable deep resonance <like a machine's burring>."[29] Their glamour, which endowed the sipping of tea with a "magic relish" in *Sisters,* now awakes a "fatal desire," so that the attraction Gudrun feels becomes the sign of a mutual fatality. Finally, the chapter ending tips the scales from realism toward myth by implying that the "secret" or cause of the destructiveness of Beldover lies in "a sort of rottenness in the will" that the miners and Gudrun share.

The failure of sympathy toward the miners can be seen clearly if one compares a late essay, "Nottingham and the Mining Countryside" (1929), with Birkin's scorn of the colliers who want pianofortes in their parlors. In the essay Lawrence defends them from middle-class snobbery by asking rhetorically, "what is a piano, often as not, but a blind reaching out for beauty."[30] To Birkin, however, the collier reaches out solely in a spirit of emulation: "It makes him so much higher in his neighbouring collier's eyes" (106). Birkin does not speak for Lawrence, but it is revealing that Lawrence does not qualify Birkin's remark with another view of the colliers' lives.

The aesthetic reason for the unconvincing portrait of the miners, in short, is that Lawrence does not give them imaginative life and does not show them choosing their fate among other possible fates as Gerald vividly chooses his. In a series of dramatic scenes, Gerald subdues life merely for the sake of exercising his will, with no redeeming purpose. Therefore it is imaginatively credible that for him "The subjugation itself was the point. . . . What he wanted was the pure fulfillment of his own will in the struggle with the natural conditions" (296). His earlier mastering of the mare and subsequent throttling of Bismarck the rabbit lend plausibility to the summary. He derives perverse satisfaction from manipulating and being manipulated by Gudrun, thereby enacting in private life his treatment of the miners. In contrast, the miners exist solely en masse, their lives summarized rather than dramatized. As a result the artistically beneficent tension between conscious hostility and unconscious sympathy for the miners in *Sons and Lovers* dissolves into almost complete repugnance. Whereas the dark vitality of Walter Morel flows intermittently into the Morel family, the potency of the "underworld, half-automatized colliers" in *Women in Love* gives off a "disruptive force" in Beldover. The myth relegates them to the underworld from which they cannot emerge as can the Plutonic figures in other Lawrentian fictions, such as the Italian Ciccio in *The Lost Girl* or the gipsy in *The Virgin and the Gipsy*.

Yet Lawrence's myth of industry has proved true to one aspect of work in the modern industrial state. In a recent poem by Philip Levine titled "Every Blessed Day," for example, a son evokes the "prison" of work from which his dead father escaped in "suspended moments" of memory. The son's life is "lost," one eternal day like that of his fellow workers in an automobile plant, where repetitiveness masks their discontents even from themselves.[31] Finally, whatever the shortcomings of this myth of industry, the symbolic aptness of Gerald as the god of Beldover is quite unlike the rhetorical insistence on Anton Skrebensky's representativeness in *The Rainbow*. Gerald's fate prefigures that of England.

"Water-Party" The annual festival held by the Crich family on Willey Water is the counterpart to Hermione Roddice's houseparty in

116

"Breadalby," which culminates in attempted murder. As in the earlier chapter, ritual elements are suffused with ominous effects. The bourgeoisie at play are watched enviously by common people outside the fence who have not been admitted to "paradise" (222), but the Brangwen sisters escape from the crowd to a secluded island where they can swim naked, "like nymphs" (230). While Ursula sings an "incantation," Gudrun dances eurythmically with "unconscious ritualistic suggestion," drawing an audience of wild bullocks. Into this idyllic scene Birkin and Gerald intrude in a less welcome repetition of the sisters observing Gerald swimming in "Diver." Both Gudrun's dance before the bullocks and the ensuing conversation and blow are mythical projections far more than realistic actions. As in Greek tragedy, specifically Euripides' *The Bacchae,* women who are engaged in private assembly and worship resent the prying of men and show their displeasure by attacking the men's cattle. Like the Bacchantes in Euripides, Gudrun dances in an abandoned posture—head flung back, throat lifted, and hair streaming—as though she is "trying to throw off some bond." Suddenly she sees the bullocks watching her, and instead of heeding Ursula's warning she turns on the animals "as if she were confident of some secret power in herself, and had to put it to the test." A scream like that of a "seagull" signals this ecstatic moment, as it had her appreciation of Gerald on the mare in "Coal-Dust" and as it will her response to Gerald's subduing of Bismarck in "Rabbit." The magical dance of intimidation is for her a "voluptuous ecstasy" compounded of "fear and pleasure." When Gerald intervenes to save her from danger, she fiercely resents his intrusion and, in revenge, rushes headlong at the cattle. Since Gerald owns the cattle, Gudrun is symbolically attacking him, as their conversation makes clear:

> "You think I'm afraid of you and your cattle, don't you?" she asked. . . .
> "Why should I think that?" he asked. . . .
> She leaned forward and swung round her arm, catching him a blow on the face with the back of her hand.
> "That's why," she said. (236)

Gerald maintains his composure, even though a "reservoir of black anger" has burst within him, remarking, "You have struck the first blow"—to which she retorts, "And I shall strike the last." Gudrun retains the advantage when Gerald avows love not anger at her willful conduct. And finally their scene ends with a reminder, mysteriously apposite, that Gerald killed his brother and "was set apart, like Cain" (238).

The interpretive possibilities here are almost endless. To pursue the mythic, we may notice that Gudrun does administer the last blow to Gerald, who by then feels like a "victim that is torn open and given to the heavens" (543), as is Pentheus in Euripides' drama or a host of dying gods in Frazer's *The Golden Bough*. As a revision suggests, Gerald's prophetic exclamation seems to be extorted from him by Gudrun in a psychic projection: "'You have struck the first blow,' he said at last, forcing the words from his lungs <, in a voice so soft and low, it sounded like a dream within her, not spoken in the outer air>."[32]

We may wonder whether the myth of Artemis (Diana) the huntress and Actaeon adds a premonition of Gudrun's ultimate victory over Gerald. In that myth, the hunter Actaeon comes upon Artemis bathing naked. As a punishment the goddess turns him into a stag and his own hounds tear him to pieces. Are we meant to notice that bullocks are castrated bulls and to recall their condition much later when Gudrun, rejecting Gerald's overbearing masculinity, thinks "Nothing is so boring as the phallus" (563)? In "Diver" Ursula remarks humorously that Gerald swimming looks "like a Nibelung," a mythical king of the dwarfs in Wagner's *Ring* cycle, one of whom appears at the bottom of the Rhine river. Now, as Gerald dives in a vain attempt to rescue his sister, Gudrun sees him in a symbolic double take. At first she is fascinated by his "loins, white and dimly luminous," which suggest that he is not a man but "an incarnation, a great phase of life" (248–49). It is a moment recalling many in *The Rainbow* when one of the Brangwen forebears sees the "otherness" of a proper mate. But here Gudrun knows that "she would never go beyond him," that she will be denied the experience of the beyond that had always replenished her Brangwen forebears. Then, after his second dive, Gerald appears defeated, "like a dumb beast" who must admit the Crich family's fatal incapacity to change, so different from the resilience of the Brangwen generations. Gudrun is left feeling isolated on the surface of the "unliving" water.

As the dragging and then draining of the lake proceeds, the life-giving, resuscitating powers of water appear to drain away too. Rains, floods, tumult in nature have occurred before in the Brangwensaga: Tom drowns in a flood, and Ursula miscarries after her encounter with the wild horses on a rain-swept common. "There was a saying that the Brangwens always died a violent death," we are reminded after the patriarch's drowning in *The Rainbow*. But the aftermath has always been reassuring, with the promise that human life is reinvigorated by nature even through death. Thus the "inviolable body" of Tom evokes feelings of "majesty" and "awe." Has water in *Women in Love* become a forbidding element in which one drowns or freezes? The "reservoir of black anger" in Gerald revealed by Gudrun's blow, for example, has links to the drowning, diving, and draining that follow and perhaps also to the later death of Mr. Crich, whose last words are a question about the draining of Willey Water to stop a leak into the pits (417). Does death itself appear solely fearful, a baleful portent rather than a marking of continuity, as in Gerald's reflections on its absolute difference from life? The answers to such questions will be different for every reader and perhaps on every rereading.

"Rabbit" and "Threshold"

While subduing the rabbit Gerald and Gudrun conduct a parody of the *Blutbrüderschaft* Birkin has urged on Gerald in "Man to Man." The setting of a civilized country house with gardens, a French governess, and a tame animal who can be viewed and sketched for a child's pastime recalls the ambience of Breadalby. In Gerald's world as in Hermione's, rituals end in cruelty and violence that reflect the suppressed feelings of the participants. Until now, with the exception of the "light blow" in "Water-Party,"

Gerald and Gudrun have not consciously admitted the violence in their attraction. Lawrence's art indirectly suggests increasing pressure—until here, the joint action of subduing Bismarck forces on the lovers a recognition: "Gudrun looked at Gerald with strange, darkened eyes, strained with underworld knowledge, almost supplicating, like those of a creature which is at his mercy, yet which is his ultimate equal. He did not know what to say to her. He felt the mutual hellish recognition. And he felt he ought to say something, to cover it. He had the power of lightning in his nerves, she seemed like a soft recipient of his magical, hideous white fire. He was unconfident, he had qualms of fear" (316–17).

But has the preparation been sufficient to validate what might seem, taken in isolation, rhetorical overkill? The passage serves as a catalyst for memories of the terrified mare at Gerald's mercy; of Gerald's northern electric force undercut by "qualms of fear" and incapacity, as when he appears to Gudrun an "amphibious beast" after failing to rescue his drowned sister; and, finally, of the attractive yet repulsive "underworld" miners. Both partners are "initiate" but Gerald feels "as if she had hit him across the face," as she had in "Water-Party" and will again at the climax in "Snowed Up." The implication that their relationship will never reach equilibrium or equality was strengthened in the second edition, where "ultimate equal" became "ultimate victor."

Slangy dialogue with an undertow in "Threshold" balances the portentous analysis of subconscious urges in "Rabbit." Mockery of Birkin's often ridiculous manner of posing ideas on marriage comes to seem a sinister gaiety masking cynicism:

> "He says," [Gudrun] added, with a grimace of irony, "that you can find an eternal equilibrium in marriage, if you accept the unison, and still leave yourself separate, don't try to fuse."
>
> "Doesn't inspire me," said Gerald.
>
> "That's just it," said Gudrun.
>
> "I believe in love, in a real *abandon*, if you're capable of it," said Gerald.

"So do I," said she.

"And so does Rupert, too—though he is always shouting."

"No," said Gudrun. "He won't abandon himself to the other person. . . ."

"Yet he wants marriage!—Marriage—et puis?"

"Le Paradis!" mocked Gudrun. (371)

Here the revised style perfectly mimes the theme. Gudrun and Gerald are split personalities, cynical about expressing their whole selves. Their ritual actions—like the later games of Gudrun and Loerke—are played with an ominous lightheartedness. It is clear that the rituals do not express their instinctual natures; that their impulses are bottled up and likely at some moment of "abandon" to shatter their worldly exteriors.

"Death and Love" The irony of the title, which reverses a romantic formula, implies that the sexual consummation of Gerald and Gudrun is implicated in the death of Mr. Crich. Their consummation also contrasts with that of Birkin and Ursula in the previous chapter, "Excurse." At the Saracen's Head and later in Sherwood Forest, Ursula discovers in Birkin one of the sons of God for whom she has been searching since her failure with Skrebensky in *The Rainbow*. Hers is a fate that she "asks for" and "accepts in full." Their love is metaphorically both a death and a rebirth, "a perfect passing away, and at the same time the most intolerable accession into being," which fulfills them and sets them free in a relationship like that of two stars in "equilibrium."

But the consummation of the second Brangwen sister is forebodingly mixed up with death in the Crich family. Gudrun's role as tutor in art and companion to Winifred is meant to divert the child's attention from her father's terminal illness. Inevitably, however, Gudrun is drawn into the drama as a resource for Gerald, who has grimly determined to see his father's death "through," despite the warnings of his mother and his own realization that the illness is a family fatality.

Rewriting, Lawrence stressed the willful in Gerald's conduct: "Gerald would experience the whole process of slow death without wincing or flinching. ['I am the master of my fate. I am the Captain of my Soul.'] <He even triumphed in it. He somehow *wanted* this death, even forced it. It was as if he himself were dealing the death, even when he most recoiled in horror. Still, he would deal it, he would triumph through death.>"[33] That "through" recalls Gerald's refusal in "Water-Party" to come away from the scene of the drowning: "No, I'll see this job through, Rupert," which was added as a premonition.[34] Her son's perverse courage to face death spurs Mrs. Crich to sarcastic wordplay: "What have *you* got to do, [going through it all. You can do no *good!*] <seeing it through? It will see itself through. You are not needed.>"[35] The experience becomes equivocal, a triumphing through death that takes place in his "soul" and may prophesy suicide. Later, when Birkin feels disgust at the sight of Gerald's frozen corpse, we may recall Mrs. Crich's warning on seeing the youthful look on her dead husband's face: "Don't let it happen again!" Is it ironic that Gerald fulfills her warning, not by avoiding death but by registering its awfulness?

The illness and death of Mr. Crich reveal to the reader and at least subliminally to the participants the fact that the Criches have not "lived as [they] ought to have done," as Tolstoy's Ivan Ilych comes to recognize before his agonizing death.[36] In *The Death of Ivan Ilych*, disease allows Ivan to gain insight into the lies of a lifetime; he wants to communicate this to his wife and daughter before he dies, but only the servant and his young son pity him. By contrast, Mr. Crich tries to evade knowledge of his condition, fearing Gerald, who loathes his father's lingering. Lawrence dwells more than Tolstoy on the psychological roots of illness in repressed feeling, but like Tolstoy he also draws on the archaic idea of a tainted community that illness has judged as, for example, Thebes is judged by the plague in *Oedipus Rex*.[37] Such is the burden of a tellingly rewritten passage. In *Sisters* Gerald said: "I tell you what, I wouldn't mind being shot to-morrow— *or* hanged—But this lingering death business is absolutely too much for me—absolutely."[38] This became in the final typescript: "It's something you don't reckon with, you know, till it is there. And then you realise that it was there all the time—it was always there—you understand what I mean?—the possibility of this incurable illness, this slow death" (408). Finally, in the Tyrol, Gudrun's thoughts on the morning of the violent climax fulfill Gerald's premonition: "Anything might come to pass on the morrow. . . . All possibility—that was the charm to her, the lovely iridescent, indefinite charm,—pure illusion. <All possibility—because death was inevitable, and *nothing* was possible but death.>"[39]

Such a revision pinpoints the effect of the world war on Lawrence's imagination. *Women in Love* became in one sense an allegory of the war, reflecting Lawrence's conviction, corroborated by Thucydides' history of the "death agony of Athens" in the Peloponnesian War, that he was living through "the real winter of the spirit in England."[40] The volume of Thucydides saves Birkin's neck from being broken by Hermione, but England like Athens may prove a dying civilization.

After the funeral Gerald is left, as was Paul Morel in *Sons and Lovers,* facing a "void." His somnambulistic quest for Gudrun recalls Paul's predicament after his mother's death; stumbling across fields and hedges in the dark, Gerald must take a direction or drift to death. In *The Rainbow* Tom Brangwen is conscious of nothing but the roaring of the wind as he goes to court Lydia, clutching a bunch of wildflowers. Gerald too goes "automatically" but arrives in Gudrun's room like a thief in the night, tracking mud from his father's grave.

Again the interpretive possibilities are tantalizing. The primary ironies are that Gerald's daring strategem and appearance as a "supernatural being" (428) are undercut by the "void" in his personality (405) and that the effect of sexual consummation on the lovers is quite opposite. As Birkin metamorphosed into a son of God in the previous chapter, so now Gerald overcomes Gudrun's scruples by appearing with "odd supernatural steadfastness," like "the young Hermes" (429). Are we meant to pursue the matter further? Hermes was not only a divine messenger who presided over gymnastics and thievery, but also Hermes Psychopompos, "the divine Herald between two worlds," a messenger to and from the dead or ghosts.[41] Gerald communes with his father's ghost, brings mud from the grave, and later, at the climax in the Tyrol, appears so suddenly that Loerke exclaims: "*Maria!* You come like a ghost" (571). Hermes and Dionysos may be recognized as two phases of one process, that of death and rebirth. Gerald's association with Hermes would then be another double take, a revaluation of his previous appearance as Dionysos when swimming at Breadalby (159). Given the allusions to *The Bacchae* in "Water-Party," it is tempting to see Gerald as a God or divine king who must be sacrificed but whose death will not renew life. Later, just before falling to his death, he stumbles on a crucifix and, in a passage cunningly revised, turns into his own, murderous ghost: "He had a great dread of being murdered. <But it was a dread which stood outside him, like his own ghost.>"[42]

In any case, Gerald's godlike presence has already been undercut; his passion is grounded in weakness. He does not seek the "star-equilibrium" of Birkin and Ursula but "something to make good the equilibrium" within himself. Consequently, he appears to Gudrun as both lover and child, subjugating and worshiping her, pouring into her his "pent-up darkness and corrosive death" and drinking in her "living effluence" (430–31). Their passion, unlike that of Birkin and Ursula, is a bondage in which one is fulfilled at the expense of the other. What revives him seems to her "a death." Previously, embracing him under the colliery bridge, Gudrun foresees many days of "harvesting" sensual knowledge from Gerald. Such language echoes but revalues that in *The Rainbow,* for Gudrun fears reaching "the end," using up rather than replenishing love. In the morning she pretends Gerald is a workman dressing for work, but she cannot overcome her feeling of nausea.

Tragedy in the Tyrol The self-destructiveness of their relationship accelerates once they arrive in the heart of the mountains, as Lawrence underscored in revision. Gerald watches Gudrun exult in the snow, for example: "she seemed to be [fleeing from] <rushing towards> her fate [in vain] <and leaving him behind>."[43] Their love is soon reduced to a battle for power, a ruthless exercise of wills. We have been prepared for the ferocity in Gerald's northern nature, the "supernatural force" that now seems unequivocally sinister. From Gerald's initial appeal as an "unbroached, pure . . . arctic thing," we have followed his outbursts of willpower as the deus ex machina and his apparition as the desired but feared Hermes to this final apotheosis. Recognizing his intention to "destroy her rather than be denied," Gudrun fights back openly, no longer disguising the will that underlies her passion. Just as Gerald subdues the miners by treating them as instruments, so Gudrun triumphs because she can use Gerald as an "element" for her gratification. This vindictive abuse of the will is conveyed in a futuristic diction that Lawrence substituted for clichés like the biblical apple: "[He looked like a fruit made to eat. He was her apple of knowledge.] <He was wonderful like a piece of radium to her.> She felt she could [set her teeth in him and eat him to the core] <consume herself and know *all*, by means of this fatal, living metal.>"[44]

The contest is unequal; the female triumphs. Gudrun assumes the stature of a Greek heroine, Cleopatra, Eleanora Duse, or perhaps a chatelaine in the medieval tradition of courtly love—all practitioners of a "female art" that achieves "perfect knowledge in sensuous understanding" (547). Like Gudrun in a tender moment, we must feel pity for the outmatched Gerald, who remains "borné" in his attachments to society and heterosexuality. The irony and pathos of Gerald's situation is that he reveals sensitivity only after he has lost Gudrun's love. As a modern knight, he will endure contempt and denials in her service for the reward of feeling a "quickening . . . the magic of the promise" (544). His night with Gudrun in "Death and Love" gave him a "grateful self-sufficiency" that she resented. But in the Tyrol he is forced to admit that he cannot do without Gudrun as evidently she can do without him. Having exhausted his interest in the mines Gerald has no place for his *go* to go, as Gudrun earlier joked. His love has given him a wound "like an open flower," proving his humanity and giving him a tragic stature. Like his fitfully expressed love for Birkin, this masochistic delight in the "cruelest joy" with Gudrun is the last equivocation of his character and fate. As in the reversal of a tragic drama such as *Macbeth,* the novel concludes with a "falsification of expectation, so that the end comes as expected, but not in the manner expected."[45] The language and setting return us to the world of *The Rainbow,* but now irony undercuts hope. Through the wound inflicted by Gudrun, Gerald feels like a victim given to the unknown and ready "like a seed that has germinated, to issue forth in being" (543). On the final morning when he attacks Gudrun and then walks to his death, the day starts "full of a promise like spring" (568).

The Tyrol provides a fitting location for this tragic finale. Lawrence had the parallel between the geographical and thematic culmination of the affair firmly in view as he rewrote, inspired by the symbolic geography in Thomas Hardy's *Tess of the D'Urbervilles.* Tess's gradual isolation is paralleled by her movement from the ancestral Vale of Blackmoor to the wooded Chase, lush Talbothays, bleak Flintcomb-Ash, and finally sacrificial Stonehenge. At Flintcomb she notices "strange birds from behind the North Pole" that have witnessed icy cataclysms.[46] This visitation may have suggested to Lawrence the theme of human life reduced to a nonhuman level, of *Kulturträgers* transmogrified to "creatures," culminating in Loerke's dream of fear: "the world went cold, and snow fell everywhere, and only white creatures, polar-bears, white foxes, and men like awful white snow-birds, persisted in ice cruelty" (552).

Like Tess Durbeyfield, Gerald undergoes a progressive alienation from society. His journey to death in a mountain pass near a crucifix resembles Tess's journey to Stonehenge and the hangman. But Aeschylean gods do not sport with Gerald as they do with poor Tess. Gerald's fate is chosen, his death a suicide. He resembles a blinded Samson pulling down the temple of European culture on everyone's head, as a subtle revision, alluding to Milton's poem *Samson Agonistes,* suggests: "Gerald . . . was intense and gripped [upon himself, like a young victor] <into white light, agonistes.>"[47]

17

Loerke, Gudrun, and the Life of an Artist

Loerke seems well adapted to the Tyrol and survives the contest with Gerald for Gudrun's affections, though Gudrun has not quite accepted his invitation to set up shop in Germany or to consider him her *Glücks-ritter*. His role as a competitor to Gerald was part of the original conception of "The Sisters." There is, however, no mention of his Jewishness then (1913) or until additions to the last version of *Women in Love* (1917 or 1919). His diverse roles as modernist artist, homosexual, and Jew have vexed critics. The manuscripts reveal several figures in the carpet.

In *Sisters*, Birkin remarked on Loerke with more hatred than clarity:

> "Look at him, Loerke. He keeps himself perfectly intact, perfectly unchanged, he makes no connection with anything whatsoever. . . . He uses other living beings to send a sensation and a warmth and a satisfaction through his glassy shell, into the horrible mess inside him—really like an insect on the living body of man."
>
> "But why does anybody submit their living body to him?" asked Gerald.

"Because they want to—they want to be devoured in that
way—it is a form of sensationalism—it satisfies them."[1]

A late revision of the above passage, which runs from "And what *is*
the end?" to "he's the wizard rat that swims ahead" (522–23), elimi-
nates the bizarre imagery of beetles that has no previous reference in
the novel.[2]

The resulting exchange is highly compact. It stresses general com-
plicity in the process of modern "corruption." Just as the African statue
in "Moony" represents "that which was imminent in [Birkin]," so the
degradation at which Loerke excels is secretly desired by all Europeans.
Loerke's background as an impoverished "mud child" lends plausibility to his hatred of social ideals such as class or nationalism. He has
wandered through Europe as a beggar and acquired polyglot fluency.
All Europe has gone into his making, as Marlow says of Kurtz in *Heart
of Darkness*.

Moreover, Birkin's striking image of Loerke as the "wizard rat"
gnawing at the roots of life is appropriate to the antipastoral setting
of the Tyrol. As one critic has noted, "the rat is the creature most
appropriate to the demonic" and consequently is omnipresent in the
memoirs and poetry of the world war, where pastoral images are
inverted to describe a landscape of utter destruction.[3] Similarly, the
Brangwensaga begins with a pastoral vision of man and beast in harmony with the earth and cycle of seasons, but ends with an antipastoral
vision of men turned to "creatures" in a frozen landscape.

But why must Loerke be "a Jew—or part Jewish"? In a letter to
the Jewish painter Mark Gertler, whose futuristic *Merry-Go-Round*
was the inspiration for Loerke's frieze, Lawrence explained the place
of the Jew in his image of contemporary history: "It would take a Jew
to paint this picture. It would need your national history to get you
here, without disintegrating you first. You are of an older race than I,
and in these ultimate processes, you are beyond me, older than I am.
But I think I am sufficiently the same, to be able to understand. . . .
And it will be left for the Jews to utter the final and great death-cry of

this epoch: the Christians are not reduced sufficiently."[4] Lawrence's only European biographer assumes that this decision to make Loerke's race an issue in Birkin's theorizing must be understood in the context of anti-Semitism like that of the contemporary writers Houston Chamberlain and Otto Weininger.[5] But surely Lawrence's racial theorizing is not of the same stripe. Chamberlain, who became Richard Wagner's son-in-law and wrote the racist *Foundations of the Nineteenth Century* (1899), condemned the Jew as an alien, subversive element in Teutonic national cultures. In sharp contrast, Lawrence admired what he imagined to be the anarchic, antinationalistic spirit of the Jews. Moreover, unlike his Anglo-American contemporaries T. S. Eliot and Ezra Pound, Lawrence saw no difference between Jews and other European races in regard to their sponsorship of materialism and dissociated intellectuality against the Lawrentian virtues of the body and blood consciousness.[6] To Birkin all Europeans are "*fleurs du mal*," involved in the process of "devolution."

The key point, then, is the acknowledgment by Birkin that Loerke is, like Conrad's Nostromo, one of us. The manuscripts reveal Lawrence's struggle to make this point. As we have noted, Loerke's origin as "part Jewish" was added to the text quite late. In *Sisters* (1916), the penultimate version, Birkin not only omits mention of Loerke's Jewishness but also denies any affinity between himself and the artist. There the personal pronoun "they" implies that Loerke appeals to others but not to Gerald or Birkin. Then in the final manuscript (1917 or 1919), Birkin speculates on Loerke's Jewishness for the first time, finding a similarity between Gerald and the artist but still denying any likeness to himself:

> "I don't understand your terms, really," Gerald said in a flat, doomed voice. "But it sounds like a rum sort of [satisfaction] <desire>."
> <"I suppose you want the same," said Birkin. "Only you want to take a quick jump downwards, in a sort of ecstasy—and he ebbs with the stream, the sewer stream.">[7]

That is the text in the Seltzer first edition. In the English edition, however, "you" became "we": "I suppose *we* want the same. . . . Only *we* want to take a quick jump downwards" (emphasis added). The change of a pronoun may seem a small point, but it demonstrates the ambiguous attraction of Loerke and his representative status.

Drama swirls around the wizardly artist. His presence fascinates Gudrun for several reasons. After a few weeks of make-believe honeymoon, she has grown tired of Gerald's masculine displays in the bedroom and elsewhere. Loerke's sexually undemanding appreciation of her beauty offers welcome relief. Like Loerke, she too has wandered and feels deracinated. Anxious to believe that her art can thrive despite the aimlessness and growing cynicism of her life, she endorses Loerke's modernist notions that a work of art bears no relation to either the artist or the world, that a *Kunstwerk* creates its own "world" apart from vulgar reality. Hence she resents Ursula's indignant, amateur opinion that Loerke's statue of a horse reflects his personality. "This horse," Ursula tells Loerke, "is a picture of your own stock, stupid brutality" (526). Are readers meant to agree with Ursula? Or is it the artist's responsibility to record the truth of the modern condition? If so, might not the horse and the gigantic frieze appear truthful records rather than bad art? The letter to Gertler, quoted above, suggests that Lawrence was not as naive as Ursula, though he too was repelled by the human truth Gertler captures on canvas. As it happens, Ursula has guessed right about Loerke's treatment of the girl model, whom he loved and tortured and then ignored. Loerke finds sexually mature women of "no use" in his art or life. Again, how are readers to judge this preference? Is it to be repudiated, seen as symptomatic of the modern age, or accorded no more significance than Loerke gives it— *peu de rapport* (546)?

More generally, how does one make art in a world where people, not only men, are reduced to "creatures"? We appreciate Gudrun's predicament and that of the woman artist, though we may question her jump to the conclusion that the artist's personality and the artifact have nothing to do with each other—a conclusion ominously similar to Gerald's earlier decision to eliminate human considerations from industrial management.

Despite Loerke's puny physique and unromantic notions of women, he emerges victorious in the contest with Gerald for Gudrun's allegiance. The irony is that Gerald's physical distaste for the "insect" is at odds with a shared vision of man's place in the modern world. After all, Loerke's art expresses Gerald's vision of the industrial world in which man is worked by the machine with the consequences, as Uncle Tom in *The Rainbow* foresaw, that marriage and sex become a "side-show," love is dissociated from work or perversely sublimated, and personal relationships offer no transcendence: "There was no going beyond [Loerke]" (522).

Indeed, the manuscript highlights the link between painter and industrialist. Having nearly finished the penultimate version, *Sisters,* Lawrence saw Mark Gertler's *Merry-Go-Round,* with its absolutely "modern" combination of "violent mechanized rotation" and "mindless human intensity of sensational extremity."[8] At once he rewrote the description of Loerke's frieze:

> [a village attacked by wolves, great naked men, ten feet high, fighting with a herd of wolves, and women running, falling, and a rush of wolves sweeping all like a storm driving in a shaggy whirl across the whole frieze.]
> <a fair, with peasants and artisans in an orgy of enjoyment, drunk and absurd in their modern dress, whirling ridiculously in round-abouts, gaping at shows, kissing and staggering and rolling in knots, swinging in swing-boats, and firing down shooting-galleries, a frenzy of chaotic motion.>[9]

The revised passage is not a verbal copy of Gertler's futuristic painting but an insight into human relations that Lawrence perceived in the painting.[10] The description may remind one of a modern version of genre paintings by Brueghel depicting peasant life. In any case, the revision was a great improvement because, unlike the farfetched symbolism of wolves, it leads to a discussion of machines and work. The frenzy of motion in the frieze is "chaotic" rather than organic. Gudrun's admiration may be an admission that mechanized labor is the social expression of her treatment of Gerald as an instrument, which in turn imitates Gerald's treatment of her. The reader, though not Gerald, recognizes that the frieze is a fitting aesthetic expression of a deus ex machina.

Gudrun is finally drawn to what one critic has called Loerke's "repleteness" or narcissism, his indifference to the outside world, his refusal to worry about the modern condition of dissociated sensibility.[11] Loerke lives in his work. Having neither full name nor lineage, he can slip through the net of class. He is self-created, an orphan like Birkin, free from the past as Ursula longs to be. In comparison to the alternately domineering and dependent Gerald, Loerke frees Gudrun's imagination: "She was happy like a child." With Loerke she can treat life as a game and her future path as pure chance: "*Wohin?* What a lovely word! She *never* wanted it answered" (570). As Birkin is sometimes tempted to do, she wants to pursue life as a picaresque novel, but unlike Birkin or her sister she must do so in isolation. From the start of the novel, Gudrun has been looking diffidently for a man. Even while rejecting Gerald, she envies Birkin and Ursula the "wonderful stability of marriage" (466) and argues for the "old connection" with home against her sister's desire to follow Birkin into exile (533). This ambivalence, her vacillation between a desire for freedom and a desire for security, is also expressed in her art. In contrast to the large-scale projects of Loerke, she sculpts small, primitive-looking figures. When viewing and judging people, similarly, she delights in reduction and satire. Adjectives such as "complete," "final," "labelled," "summed up," and "placed forever" modify her acts of perception. Her remarks and anecdotes run to sarcasm, as in her mockery of Birkin's ideas of marriage ("Threshold") or her narrative of a detestable ride on a Thames steamer ("Water-Party"). In sum, there seems to be an underlying fear and want in Gudrun that a life like Loerke's will neither ease nor fulfill. That is the pathos of her unresolved fate. She has survived, but to what end? *Wohin?*

18

"Exeunt": Ending as Beginning

"Exeunt" provides two endings to the novel. Whereas the Crich family history and the relationship of Gerald and Gudrun have ends, the marriage of Birkin and Ursula remains open to the future. Their ongoing debate about other, "additional" forms of "eternal union" may be spirited enough to arrest the drift toward death. Put another way, the endings renew the double motion of change and continuity that characterizes the whole Brangwensaga. Whereas Gerald and Gudrun reach a tragic climax in an antipastoral setting that ironically recalls the pastoral opening of *The Rainbow,* Birkin and Ursula will seek a landscape of desire by "hop[ping] off" the world. That movement becomes the characteristic method of closure in Lawrence's subsequent fiction. Alvina Houghton of *The Lost Girl,* for example, is relieved to see the "ash-grey coffin" of England sink into the sea as she sails for Italy, though on arrival in the mountain village of Pescocalascio she finds, as Birkin forewarns Ursula, that even for such lovers as Romeo and Juliet "a fearfully cold wind blows" in Italy. In terms of narrative structure, Lawrence's innovation was to question both the finality of the end and also the ease of beginning again. Any easy recourse to escapism is checked by Birkin's thoughts at the site of Gerald's death.

Even if Gerald had found the rope and climbed over the mountain, he could not have escaped his character and tragic fate: "And what then? The Imperial road! The south? Italy? What then? Was it a way out?— It was only a way in again" (579–80).

It is not surprising that Lawrence had great trouble deciding on a fitting end. He had begun with the story of *Women in Love*, only to find that he must proceed backwards, writing generation before generation until he had created the historical vantage from which to understand the contemporary world. Having created the first generations of the Brangwens, he had to split the unwieldy saga into two novels. So the end of *The Rainbow*, having become yet another beginning, had to be left open, promising development rather than completion. Hence Lawrence tinkered at the last paragraph in proof, adding the final sentence that prophesies "the world built up in a living fabric of Truth, fitting to the overarching heaven."[1]

But the dire condition of the modern world in *Women in Love* will not permit Ursula or Birkin to envision Beldover transformed as Ursula had seen the earth cleansed of sordid habitations and assuming a "new architecture." Ursula and Lawrence have learned its intransigency and the need to escape for a time. Nevertheless, when Lawrence declared in a letter of July 1917 that "in the world of Europe I see no Rainbow . . . no Ararat will rise above the subsiding iron water," and that consequently *Women in Love* is "purely destructive, not like *The Rainbow*, destructive-consummating," he was forgetting momentarily that the New World "isn't really a locality" but a "perfected relation."[2] Although "Exeunt" doesn't reach for a symbolic ending comparable to Ursula's rainbow, it allows us to believe that the regeneration of mankind may begin in the ongoing love of Birkin and Ursula.

How to conclude puzzled Lawrence even as he finished the first draft of the novel in 1916. To his literary agent he promised "the last chapter, which, being a sort of epilogue, I want to write later."[3] A page of this abandoned epilogue survives. The time is one year after the death of Gerald. Gudrun writes to Ursula from Frankfurt announcing the birth of Ferdinand Gerald Crich who has "the limbs and body of his father" and hair "like the sun shining."[4] Lawrence was recalling the plot of the very first version of "The Sisters," in which Gudrun is pregnant with Gerald's child.

Surely Lawrence was wise to abandon the Victorian convention of an epilogue or final chapter predicting the future of the characters. (The alternative endings of *Great Expectations* and "Aftercourses" of *The Return of the Native* provide examples.) The thought of Gudrun Brangwen pursuing her fate as both mother and artist might have tested the reader's credulity. Unlike Birkin or Ursula, Gudrun seems to have "finished" with the attempt to live through love. For better or worse, she has reached an end to the Brangwen quest for a son of God and a utopian marriage. She has embarked, alone, on a different, unforseeable journey. For Ursula and Birkin too the future remains open, the story unfinished, the ideal of "a little freedom with people" unrealized.

In fact, three possible endings to the story of Birkin and Ursula survive in the manuscripts. All center on Birkin's return and lamentation over Gerald's body, but only the final has the conversation between Birkin and Ursula at the Mill. In both earlier versions, which end in the Tyrol, Birkin's grief is excessive. His broken and tearful address to Gerald's corpse alternates between hope and despair for himself. Birkin's breakdown recalls that of Paul Morel at the death of Gertrude Morel in *Sons and Lovers*. The deathbed scenes have both men "whisper" to the beloved corpse. In early endings of *Women in Love*, however, Birkin's grief is even sharper than Paul's because Birkin has never expressed openly his love for Gerald, as Paul expresses love for his mother. *Sisters*, the penultimate version, was reticent on the subject of *Blutbrüderschaft;* male love remained almost wholly suppressed. As a result, Birkin's complete collapse seemed not only sentimental but confusing, leaving the reader bewildered and more skeptical of the redeeming values in his love for Ursula. A few excerpts from the concluding paragraphs of *Sisters* will suggest the irresolute conception of this ending:

> Birkin's grief was chiefly misery. He could not bear that the beautiful, virile Gerald was a heap of inert matter, a transient heap, rubbish on the face of the earth, really. . . .
> Birkin's heart was frozen as he went back. How can one

judge—we are *not* masters of our fate—we die as we are born, uncreated or created. . . .

"Never mind, Gerald," he murmured, "never mind. Perhaps it had to be like this. It needn't destroy that which *does* live—why should it?" The tears rose again. "I *did* want it to come right for us all, I did want you to be happy, I *didn't* want you to be alone, and die. . . . But perhaps this was the only way—this nothingness—perhaps it was. Perhaps something *must* be a living nothingness. . . . —Only it seems so *empty*, so nothing—it all seems *nothing*—". . . . He could not bear it. His heart seemed to be torn in his chest.

"But even then," he strove to say, "we needn't all be like that. All is not lost, because many are lost.—I am not afraid or ashamed to die and be dead."[5]

In the final version, by contrast, Gerald turns from a transient heap of matter into a symbolic apotheosis of the northern way. The living Gerald who resented the "terrible," "abstracted" face of the African fetish statue has frozen into a northern fetish statue on which Birkin looks with terror and pity. This echo of the meditation in "Moony" makes Gerald's fate seem, if not predestined, at least intelligible. Instead of vacillating between chance and fate, Birkin sees clearly that Gerald, even if he had found "a way out" over the snow wall, would not have found a purpose to his life or a vital use of his "go." Because Birkin can face this human truth unflinchingly, he can meditate on history without rancor. Whereas originally he was overwhelmed by the fact of Gerald's death and unable to draw a moral, now he returns to the ideas of "An Island" and "Water-Party": "Whatever the mystery which has brought forth man, it is a non-human mystery." Man may have failed creatively to develop, as the ichthyosauri or mastodons failed. Gerald, the deus ex machina of England, is such a modern creature. But we may hope that the nonhuman mystery will express itself in a "new, more lovely race."

In the original version Birkin feels "frozen by the death that possessed himself, as well as Gerald." When he breaks into tears, Ursula is "aghast" and slips from the room to spare herself the sight.

In the final version, however, Ursula remains, though unsympathetic at first. Her skeptical presence during the lamentation and her sharp question—"What difference would it [Gerald's loving Birkin] have made?"—save Birkin from fatalism. When he turns to the "cold, mute, material" face, he sees "Gerald! the Denier!" who chose death. He remembers their last handclasp, "a warm, momentaneous grip of final love. For one second—then let go again, let go forever." The memory is moving because it captures the blend of warmth and reserve in Gerald's nature, recalling earlier handclasps in "Water-Party" and "Gladiatorial."

Thus the final version does not end, as the original had, with Birkin alone beside the corpse, proclaiming the same courage to die that led to Gerald's suicide. Instead, Ursula's down-to-earth "You've got me" leads the couple to affirm their love in the face of death. It is a love that will grow through spirited debate. Thus the coda opens out the novel, leaving the reader with subtly posed but unresolved questions about life. It is pleasing to note that "THE END," with which the novel ended in its first edition, was not written by Lawrence but by the publisher. Now *Women in Love* ends, as Lawrence intended, by questioning the finality of life and art: "'I don't believe that,' he answered."

Notes and References

1. Composition

1. F. R. Leavis, *D. H. Lawrence: Novelist* (Harmondsworth: Penguin, 1964), 15.

2. *The Letters of D. H. Lawrence,* ed. James T. Boulton, 8 vols. (Cambridge: Cambridge University Press, 1979–), 1:503; hereafter cited as *Letters.*

3. Ibid., 1: 427.

4. Ibid., 2: 90.

5. *Sons and Lovers* (Harmondsworth: Penguin, 1981), 315.

6. Ibid., 381.

7. Ibid., 431.

8. Ibid., 421.

9. Charles L. Ross, *The Composition of "The Rainbow" and "Women in Love": A History* (Charlottesville: University Press of Virginia, 1979).

10. *Letters,* 1: 546.

11. Ibid., 2: 165.

12. Robert Lynd, review of *The Rainbow* in *Daily News,* 5 October 1915; reprinted in *D. H. Lawrence: The Critical Heritage,* ed. R. P. Draper (London: Routledge & Kegan Paul, 1970), 92.

13. *Letters,* 2: 233.

14. Robert Wohl, *The Generation of 1914* (Cambridge: Harvard University Press, 1979), 210.

15. Ibid., 229.

16. "Morality and the Novel," in *Phoenix I: The Posthumous Papers of D. H. Lawrence,* ed. Edward D. McDonald (London: Heinemann, 1936), 528.

17. "Why the Novel Matters," in *Phoenix I,* 535.

2. The Importance of the Work

1. *Letters,* 3: 459.

2. Leavis, *D. H. Lawrence: Novelist,* 99 and 101.

3. Harold Bloom, "Poetry, Revisionism, Repression," *Critical Inquiry* 2 (Winter 1975):234.

4. "Foreword to *Women in Love,*" in *Phoenix II: Uncollected, Unpublished, and Other Prose Works of D. H. Lawrence,* ed. Warren Roberts and Harry T. Moore (London: Heinemann, 1968), 276.

5. Leavis, *D. H. Lawrence: Novelist,* 15.

6. Samuel Taylor Coleridge, *Biographia Literaria,* ed. George Watson (London: Dent, 1956), 174.

7. David Lodge, "D. H. Lawrence: Genius, Heretic, Classic," in *Write On: Occasional Essays, 1965–85* (London: Secker & Warburg, 1986), 193.

8. W. B. Yeats, "Lapis Lazuli," in *Collected Poems,* ed. Richard J. Finneran (New York: Macmillan, 1983), 294–95.

3. Critical Reception

1. James Douglas and Clement Shorter, reviews of *The Rainbow* in, respectively, the *Star,* 22 October 1915, and the *Sphere,* 23 October 1915; reprinted in *The Critical Heritage,* 95–96.

2. J. M. Murry, review of *Women in Love* in the *Nation and Athenaeum,* 13 August 1921; reprinted in *The Critical Heritage,* 172.

3. Anonymous, "A Genius Pain-Obsessed," obituary in the *Manchester Guardian,* 4 March 1930; reprinted in *The Critical Heritage,* 325.

4. T. S. Eliot, "The Contemporary Novel," original English text of "Le Roman Anglais Contemporain," *La Nouvelle Revue Française,* 1 May 1927; reprinted in *The Critical Heritage,* 276.

5. Douglas, review reprinted in *The Critical Heritage,* 94.

6. Reader's report on *Women in Love* for Constable Publishers; quoted in *Women in Love,* ed. David Farmer et al. (Cambridge: Cambridge University Press, 1987), xxxiv.

7. Thomas Hardy, *Jude the Obscure,* ed. Irving Howe (Boston: Houghton Mifflin, 1965), 3–4.

8. *Letters,* 2: 132.

9. Ibid., 2: 479.

10. John Galsworthy, "Letter to J. B. Pinker," autumn 1915; reprinted in *The Critical Heritage,* 108.

Notes and References

11. Catherine Carswell, review of *The Rainbow* in the *Glasgow Herald*, 4 November 1915; reprinted in *The Critical Heritage*, 101.

12. Murry, review of *Women in Love*, reprinted in *The Critical Heritage*, 170.

13. Leavis, *D. H. Lawrence, Novelist:* 205.

14. Murry, review reprinted in *The Critical Heritage*, 171.

15. Evelyn Scott, composite review of *Women in Love* and *The Lost Girl*, in the *Dial*, April 1921; reprinted in *The Critical Heritage*, 162.

16. Angus Wilson, "At the Heart of Lawrence," *Encounter*, December 1955, 83–85; Herbert Read, "On D. H. Lawrence," *The Twentieth Century* 165 (1959):558. J. Hillis Miller, *Fiction and Repetition* (Cambridge: Harvard University Press, 1982).

17. *Letters*, 2: 182.

18. *The Collected Letters of D. H. Lawrence*, ed. Harry T. Moore, 2 vols. (London: Heinemann, 1962), 2: 799.

19. E. M. Forster, "Lawrence's Art and Ideas," the *Listener*, 30 April 1930; reprinted in *The Critical Heritage*, 346.

20. Robert Lynd, review of *The Rainbow* in the *Daily News*, 5 October 1915; reprinted in *The Critical Heritage*, 91.

21. Katherine Mansfield, *The Scrapbook of Katherine Mansfield*, ed. J. M. Murry (London: Constable, 1939), 156–157; reprinted in *The Critical Heritage*, 168.

22. Murry, review reprinted in *The Critical Heritage*, 168.

23. "We Need One Another," in *Phoenix I*, 193.

24. H. M. Swanwick, review of *The Rainbow* in the *Manchester Guardian*, 28 October 1915; reprinted in *The Critical Heritage*, 99.

25. W. C. Pilley, *John Bull*, 17 September 1921; reprinted in *D. H. Lawrence: A Critical Anthology*, ed. H. Coombes (Harmondsworth: Penguin 1973), 145.

26. T. S. Eliot, review in *Criterion*, July 1931; reprinted in *The Critical Heritage*, 359.

27. Philip Callow, *The Young D. H. Lawrence* (New York: Stein and Day, 1975), 12.

28. Aldous Huxley, "Introduction," 1932; reprinted in *Collected Letters*, ed. Moore, 2: 1254.

29. *Letters*, 1: 544.

30. Frank Kermode, *Lawrence* (London: Fontana/Collins, 1973), 7.

31. *Studies in Classic American Literature* (Harmondsworth: Penguin, 1971), 8.

32. Michael Levenson, "'The Passion of Opposition' in *Women in Love:* None, One, Two, Few, Many," *Modern Language Studies* 17 (Spring 1987):35.

4. "Prologue": An Abandoned Beginning

1. "Prologue," in *Phoenix II,* 103–04.

2. Timothy d'Arch Smith, *Love in Earnest: Some Notes on the Lives and Writings of English "Uranian" Poets from 1889–1930* (London: Routledge & Kegan Paul, 1970), 191–93.

3. "Prologue," in *Phoenix II,* 98–99.

4. George H. Ford, ed., " 'The Wedding' Chapter of D. H. Lawrence's *Women in Love,"* *Texas Studies in Language and Literature* 6 (1964):134–47.

5. "Sisters": Beginning as Ending

1. Quoted in Bloom, "Poetry, Revisionism, Repression," 237.

2. Hugh Kenner, "The *Portrait* in Perspective," in James Joyce, *A Portrait of the Artist as a Young Man,* ed. Chester G. Anderson (New York: Viking, 1968), 418.

3. *Letters,* 1: 477.

4. Carolyn Heilbrun, "Marriage Perceived: English Literature 1873–1941," in *What Manner of Woman,* ed. Marlene Springer (New York: New York University Press, 1977), 176.

5. Ibid.

6. Ibid., 175.

7. *Study of Thomas Hardy,* in *Phoenix I,* 413.

8. Heilbrun, "Marriage Perceived," 180.

6. "Remarkable Females": Lawrence and Women

1. "Daughters of the Vicar," *The Complete Short Stories of D. H. Lawrence,* 3 vols. (New York: Viking, 1961), 1:145.

2. *The Lost Girl,* ed. John Worthen (Cambridge: Cambridge University Press, 1981), 83.

3. Ibid., 273.

4. *The Rainbow,* ed. John Worthen (Harmondsworth: Penguin, 1981), 487.

5. Thomas Hardy, *Tess of the D'Urbervilles,* ed. William E. Buckler (Boston: Houghton Mifflin, 1960), 202.

6. Charles L. Ross, "D. H. Lawrence and Greek Tragedy: Euripides and Ritual," *D. H. Lawrence Review* 10 (Spring 1977): 1–19.

7. "The Novel," in *Phoenix II,* 416. The affair between Anna Karenina and cavalry captain Vronsky was clearly one source of Ursula's affair with Skrebensky, an officer in the Royal Engineers and a horseman whose "muscles developed very strong through riding" appeal to Ursula. Barbara Hardy compares Vronsky's breaking a mare's back during a steeplechase and Gerald's subduing an Arab mare at the railroad crossing in "Coal-Dust." See Barbara Hardy, *The Appropriate Form* (London: Athlone Press, 1964), 179.

7. Marriage

1. *The Rainbow,* ed. John Worthen (Harmondsworth: Penguin, 1981), 140.

2. Ibid., 165.

3. Ibid., 325.

4. Ibid., 248–49.

5. Ibid., 281.

6. Charles L. Ross, "The Revisions of the Second Generation in *The Rainbow,*" *Review of English Studies* 27 (1976):277–95.

7. *The Rainbow,* 545.

8. *Collected Letters,* ed. Moore, 2: 990.

8. History, Repetition, and Paternity

1. Ross, *The Composition of "The Rainbow" and "Women in Love,"* 82.

2. Patricia Drechsel Tobin, *Time and the Novel: The Genealogical Imperative* (Princeton: Princeton University Press, 1978), 87.

3. Edward Said, *The World, the Text, and the Critic* (Cambridge, MA: Harvard University Press, 1983), 123.

4. Ibid., 125.

5. Peter Brooks, *Reading for the Plot: Design and Intention in Narrative* (New York: Random House, 1984), 115.

6. Ian Gregor, *The Great Web: The Form of Hardy's Major Fiction* (London: Faber & Faber, 1974), 232.

7. *Letters,* 2: 181.

8. *The Rainbow,* 165.

9. Tobin, *Time and the Novel,* 12–16.

10. Frank Kermode, "Lawrence and the Apocalyptic Types," *D. H. Lawrence, "The Rainbow" and "Women in Love": A Casebook,* ed. Colin Clarke (London: Macmillan, 1969), 218.

9. Social Reality

1. *The Rainbow,* 281.

2. Joyce Carol Oates, "Lawrence's Götterdämmerung: The Tragic Vision of *Women in Love,*" *Critical Inquiry* 4 (Spring 1978): 564–65.

3. Catherine Carswell, *The Savage Pilgrimage* (London: Martin Secker, 1932), 38.

4. David Craig, *The Real Foundations* (London: Chatto & Windus, 1973), 164.

10. Structure and Characterization

1. Leavis, *D. H. Lawrence: Novelist,* 158.

2. *Study of Thomas Hardy,* in *Phoenix I,* 439.

3. "Foreword to *Women in Love,*" in *Phoenix II,* 275.

4. John Bayley, *The Characters of Love* (London: Chatto & Windus, 1960), 41.

5. Robert Langbaum, *The Mysteries of Identity: A Theme in Modern Literature* (New York: Oxford University Press, 1977), 334.

6. *Letters,* 1: 261.

7. Frank Kermode, *The Sense of an Ending* (New York: Oxford University Press, 1967), 83–84.

8. Percy Lubbock, "The Defects in *Anna Karenina,*" in Leo Tolstoy, *Anna Karenina,* ed. George Gibian (New York: W. W. Norton, 1970), 839.

11. Language, Modern Painting, and the War

1. John Berger, *About Looking* (New York: Pantheon, 1980), 6.

2. *Letters,* 2: 182–83.

3. Jack Lindsay, "The Impact of Modernism on Lawrence," in *The Paintings of D. H. Lawrence,* ed. Mervyn Levy (New York: Viking, 1964), 45.

4. Ibid., 47.

5. *The Rainbow,* 367–68.

6. *Women in Love,* corrected typescript, E441f, 634.

7. George Ford, *Double Measure: A Study of the Novels and Stories of D. H. Lawrence* (New York: Holt, Rinehart & Winston, 1965), 186. Ford lists some of Lawrence's reading in anthropology.

8. *Study of Thomas Hardy,* in *Phoenix I,* 419.

9. Ross, "The Revisions of the Second Generation in *The Rainbow,*" 285–86.

10. *The Rainbow,* 515.

11. Umberto Boccioni, "Technical Manifesto of Futurist Painting," *Umberto Boccioni,* ed. Ester Coen (New York: Metropolitan Museum of Art, 1988), 231.

12. Animals and Humans

1. *Apocalypse* (New York: Viking, 1966), 97.

2. Gilbert Murray, *Four Stages of Greek Religion* (New York: Columbia University Press, 1912), 19.

3. Berger, *About Looking,* 5.

4. "Pan in America," in *Phoenix I,* 29.

5. *The Rainbow,* 43.

6. Berger, *About Looking,* 15.

7. *St. Mawr* (New York: Random House, 1953), 19–20.

8. *Apocalypse,* 98.

9. *The Fox,* in *Four Short Novels by D. H. Lawrence* (New York: Viking, 1965), 160.

13. Sight and Touch

1. *Letters,* 2: 183.

2. "Introduction to These Paintings," in *Phoenix I,* 579.

3. Murry, review reprinted in *The Critical Heritage,* 170.

14. Dawn of the Gods: Mythic Realism

1. T. S. Eliot, "*Ulysses,* Order and Myth," *Dial* 75 (1923):481.

2. John Paterson, *The Making of "The Return of the Native"* (Berkeley: University of California Press, 1960), 127. The italicized words were added to the manuscript in revision so as to heighten the classical atmosphere. In the *Odyssey,* one of Odysseus' many shipwrecks on the way home to Ithaca occurs on the island of Phaecia, where he is much admired by lovely Nausicaa and given a ship and provisions by her father, King Alcinous.

3. Wohl, *The Generation of 1914,* 90.

4. *Letters,* 2: 330–31.

5. Richard Jenkyns, *The Victorians and Ancient Greece* (Cambridge, MA: Harvard University Press, 1980), 342.

6. The magical thighs, which appear in the first edition (published by Seltzer in America), were cut by Lawrence from the second edition (published by Secker in Britain). They are retained in my Penguin critical edition but dropped from the Cambridge critical edition. It could be argued that Lawrence had second thoughts or that he censored himself. In either case, he may have made a poor artistic choice. In my opinion, the passage not only succeeds in itself but was likely a part of Lawrence's inspiration in giving Birkin Panlike characteristics later on.

7. *The Rainbow,* 500.

8. "Pan in America," in *Phoenix I,* 22.

9. Gregory Lucente, *The Narrative of Realism and Myth: Verga, Lawrence, Faulkner, Pavese* (Baltimore: Johns Hopkins University Press, 1981), 17–20.

10. Langbaum, *The Mysteries of Identity,* 340.

15. Style

1. Laurence Lerner, *The Truthtellers* (London: Chatto & Windus, 1967), 82.

2. "Foreword to *Women in Love,*" in *Phoenix II,* 276

3. David J. Gordon, "Sex and Language in Lawrence," *Twentieth Century Literature* 27 (1981): 366.

16. Three Couples

1. *The Rainbow,* 64.

2. *Sisters,* corrected typescript, 47, located at University of Texas at Austin and listed as item E441d in Warren Roberts, *A Bibliography of D. H. Lawrence,* 2d ed. (Cambridge: Cambridge University Press, 1982).

Notes and References

3. *Movements in European History,* ed. J. T. Boulton (Oxford: Oxford University Press, 1971), 307, 310, 321.

4. Ross, *The Composition of "The Rainbow" and "Women in Love,"* 126–30.

5. Scott Sanders, *D. H. Lawrence: The World of the Five Major Novels* (New York: Viking, 1973), 131.

6. J. M. Murry, *Son of Woman* (London: Jonathan Cape, 1931), 102.

7. Jeffrey Meyers, "D. H. Lawrence and Homosexuality," *London Magazine* 13 (1973): 98.

8. *Sisters,* corrected typescript, 63–64, E441d in Warren Roberts, *A Bibliography of D. H. Lawrence.*

9. Ibid., 245.

10. Ibid., 252.

11. George Donaldson, "Men in Love? D. H. Lawrence, Rupert Birkin, and Gerald Crich," *D. H. Lawrence Centenary Essays,* ed. Mara Kalnins (Bristol, UK: Bristol Classical Press, 1986), 59.

12. Lawrence may have chosen the foreign term because he found the English connotations of homosexual both socially inadmissible and too narrow. Casual homosexual relations were as repugnant to Lawrence as heterosexual promiscuity. Charles L. Ross, "Homoerotic Feeling in *Women in Love*: Lawrence's 'struggle for verbal consciousness' in the Manuscripts," in *D. H. Lawrence: The Man Who Lived,* ed. R. B. Partlow and Harry T. Moore (Carbondale: Southern Illinois University Press, 1980), 171–72, 177.

13. Oates, "Lawrence's Götterdämmerung," 570.

14. Donaldson, "Men in Love?," 58.

15. Ross, "Homoerotic Feeling in *Women in Love,*" 180.

16. *Women in Love,* corrected typescript, 427, University of Texas at Austin, item E441f in Warren Roberts, *A Bibliography of D. H. Lawrence.*

17. Donaldson, "Men in Love?," 53.

18. *Women in Love,* corrected typescript, E441f, 642.

19. Ibid., 14.

20. Ibid., 170, 382–83.

21. *Letters,* 3: 57.

22. *Women in Love,* corrected typescript, E441f, 32.

23. For example, *The City Rises* and *Elasticity* by Umberto Boccioni (*Umberto Boccioni,* ed. Coen, 95, 156).

24. Raymond Williams, *The Country and the City* (New York: Oxford University Press, 1973), 266.

25. Craig, *The Real Foundations,* 146.

26. Ibid., 166–67.

27. Leavis, *D. H. Lawrence: Novelist*, 171.

28. *Women in Love*, corrected typescript, E441f, 177.

29. Ibid., 178.

30. "Nottingham and the Mining Countryside," in *Phoenix I*, 138.

31. Philip Levine, "Every Blessed Day," *New Yorker*, 5 December 1988, 44.

32. *Women in Love*, corrected typescript, E441f, 274.

33. Ibid., 513.

34. Ibid., 306.

35. Ibid., 521.

36. Leo Tolstoy, "The Death of Ivan Ilych," *Great Short Works of Leo Tolstoy*, ed. John Bayley (New York: Harper & Row, 1967), 295.

37. Susan Sontag, *Illness as Metaphor* (New York: Farrar, Straus & Giroux, 1978), 40.

38. *Women in Love*, corrected typescript, E441f, 517–18.

39. Ibid., 757.

40. *Letters*, 2: 393.

41. Murray, *Four Stages of Greek Religion*, 74.

42. *Women in Love*, corrected typescript, E441f, 767.

43. Ibid., 636.

44. Ibid., 634.

45. Kermode, *The Sense of an Ending*, 53.

46. Hardy, *Tess of the D'Urbervilles*, 255.

47. *Women in Love*, corrected typescript, E441f, 705.

17. Loerke, Gudrun, and the Life of an Artist

1. *Sisters*, corrected typescript, E441d, 579.

2. Ford, *Double Measure*, 198. This largely private imagery has been discussed by Ford. The associations reveal more about Lawrence's psychology during a nightmarish period in his life than about his art.

3. Paul Fussell, *The Great War and Modern Memory* (New York: Oxford University Press, 1975), 252.

4. *Letters*, 2: 660–61.

5. Emile Delavenay, *D. H. Lawrence: The Man and His Work, the Formative Years: 1885–1919*, trans. K. M. Delavenay (London: Heinemann, 1972), 298–303, 424–26.

6. Robert Alter, "Eliot, Lawrence, and the Jews: Two Versions of Europe," *Defenses of the Imagination* (Philadelphia: Jewish Publication Society, 1977), 137–51.

7. *Women in Love,* corrected typescript, E441f, 691.

8. *Letters,* 2: 660.

9. *Women in Love,* corrected typescript, E441d, 571.

10. Gertler's painting is reproduced in Marianna Torgovnick, *The Visual Arts, Pictorialism, and the Novel* (Princeton: Princeton University Press, 1985), plate 4 following p. 100.

11. Ronald Gray, "*Women in Love* and the German Tradition in Literature," in *"The Rainbow" and "Women in Love,"* ed. Clarke, 199.

18. "Exeunt": Ending as Beginning

1. Ross, *The Composition of "The Rainbow" and "Women in Love,"* 71–72.

2. *Letters,* 3: 142–43.

3. Ibid., 2: 669.

4. Ross, *The Composition,* 114.

5. *Sisters,* corrected typescript, E441d, 663–66.

Selected Bibliography

Primary Works

Fiction

The Complete Short Stories of D. H. Lawrence. 3 vols. New York: Viking, 1961.

The Escaped Cock. Edited by Gerald M. Lacy. Los Angeles: Black Sparrow Press, 1973.

The Fox in *Four Short Novels by D. H. Lawrence.* New York: Viking Press, 1965.

Kangaroo. Harmondsworth: Penguin, 1950.

The Lost Girl. Edited by John Worthen. Cambridge: Cambridge University Press, 1981.

"The Prologue to *Women in Love.*" Edited by George H. Ford. *Texas Quarterly* 6 (1963):98–111.

" 'The Wedding' Chapter of D. H. Lawrence's *Women in Love.*" Edited by George H. Ford. *Texas Studies in Literature and Language* 6 (1964): 134–47.

The Rainbow. Edited by John Worthen. Harmondsworth: Penguin, 1981.

The Rainbow. Edited by Mark Kinkead-Weekes. Cambridge: Cambridge University Press, 1989.

"St. Mawr" and "The Man Who Died." New York: Random House, 1953.

Sons and Lovers. Edited by Keith Sagar. Harmondsworth: Penguin, 1981.

Women in Love. New York: Privately Printed for Subscribers Only [Thomas Seltzer], 1920. The first edition.

Women in Love. Edited by Charles L. Ross. Harmondsworth: Penguin, 1982.

Women in Love. Edited by David Farmer, John Worthen, and Lindeth Vasey. Cambridge: Cambridge University Press, 1987.

Nonfiction

Apocalypse. New York: Viking, 1966.

Movements in European History. Edited by J. T. Boulton. Oxford: Oxford University Press, 1971.

Phoenix I: The Posthumous Papers of D. H. Lawrence. Edited by Edward D. McDonald. London: Heinemann, 1936.

Phoenix II: Uncollected, Unpublished, and Other Prose Works of D. H. Lawrence. Edited by Warren Roberts and Harry T. Moore. London: Heinemann, 1968.

Letters

The Collected Letters of D. H. Lawrence. Edited by Harry T. Moore. London: Heinemann, 1962.

The Letters of D. H. Lawrence. Edited by James T. Boulton et al. Cambridge: Cambridge University Press, 1979–.

Manuscripts

The Rainbow. Corrected typescript. E331b in Warren Roberts.

Women in Love. Corrected typescripts. E441d and E441f in Warren Roberts.

All cited manuscripts of the double novel are housed in the Humanities Research Center, University of Texas at Austin. A duplicate of *Sisters* is owned by the University of Toronto; see Ross (1979) for details.

Women in Love. London: Martin Secker, 1920. Proof, corrected and revised by Lawrence, for first English edition, published in 1921; owned by University of Texas at Austin. E441g in Warren Roberts.

Secondary Works

Bibliographies

Cowan, James C. *D. H. Lawrence: An Annotated Bibliography of Writings about Him*. 2 vols. De Kalb: Northern Illinois University Press, 1985.

Most complete listing of reviews, scholarship, adaptations, re-creations, through 1975.

Roberts, Warren. *A Bibliography of D. H. Lawrence.* 2d ed. Cambridge: Cambridge University Press, 1982. Description of all first appearances in print of Lawrence's works with notes on circumstances of composition and differences in texts; includes checklist of all known manuscripts.

Biographies

Carswell, Catherine. *The Savage Pilgrimage.* 2d ed. London: Martin Secker, 1932. The first biography, written by a friend, fellow novelist, and champion of Lawrence's work.

Delavenay, Emile. *D. H. Lawrence: The Man and His Work, the Formative Years: 1885–1919.* Translated by K. M. Delavenay. London: Heinemann, 1972. Biography by a European scholar who interviewed some of the actors in Lawrence's life drama (e.g., Jessie Chambers and Helen Corke) and who speculates on European influences; the tone, however, is frequently hostile.

E. T. [Jessie Chambers]. *D. H. Lawrence: A Personal Record.* London: Jonathan Cape, 1935. Fascinating, rival re-creation of the early years that the author, the model for Miriam Leivers, argues are distorted in *Sons and Lovers.*

Moore, Harry T. *The Priest of Love.* New York: Farrar, Straus & Giroux, 1974. The fullest life to date, though discussion of the fiction is thin.

Murry, John Middleton. *Son of Woman: The Story of D. H. Lawrence.* London: Jonathan Cape, 1931. Fascinatingly wrongheaded, psychological explanation of Lawrence's failure as man and artist; what Aldous Huxley called "destructive hagiography."

Nehls, Edward, ed. *D. H. Lawrence: A Composite Biography.* 3 vols. Madison: University of Wisconsin Press, 1957–59. Unique collection of testimonies, interviews, and written accounts by contemporaries, stitched together with excerpts from Lawrence's letters and commentary by editor.

Sagar, Keith. *D. H. Lawrence: A Calendar of His Works.* Austin: University of Texas Press, 1979. Guide to sequence of writing and painting.

———. *The Life of D. H. Lawrence.* New York: Pantheon, 1980. Brief, mostly in Lawrence's own words, and beautifully illustrated.

Schneider, Daniel J. *The Consciousness of D. H. Lawrence: An Intellectual Biography.* Lawrence, Kansas: University Press of Kansas, 1986. Intellectual biography, focusing on Lawrence's religious vision, with brief chronologies.

Selected Bibliography

Interpretations of Lawrence

Alter, Robert. *Defenses of the Imagination*. Philadelphia: Jewish Publication Society, 1977. Balanced view of Lawrence on the question of Jewishness, stressing his difference from the anti-Semitism of T. S. Eliot and Ezra Pound.

Clarke, Colin. *River of Dissolution: D. H. Lawrence and English Romanticism*. London: Routledge & Kegan Paul, 1969. The rhetoric of Romantic decadence as refashioned by Lawrence to acknowledge the attraction and even necessity of "decreation" and death in tension with the desire for renewal or rebirth; another revisionist critique of the moral and healthy Lawrence admired by F. R. Leavis; ingenious but exaggerated picture of Lawrence half in love with death.

Craig, David. *The Real Foundations*. London: Chatto & Windus, 1973. Critique of social vision in novel, informed by Marxism; a corrective to F. R. Leavis's advocacy of Lawrence as incisive social historian.

Donaldson, George. "Men in Love? D. H. Lawrence, Rupert Birkin, and Gerald Crich." In *D. H. Lawrence Centenary Essays*, edited by Mara Kalnins, 41–67. Bristol, UK: Bristol Classical Press, 1986. A debunk that claims to find confusion in Lawrence's treatment of homoeroticism where there is, in actuality, the rich ambiguity of great art.

Daleski, H. M. *The Forked Flame: A Study of D. H. Lawrence*. London: Faber & Faber, 1965. First study to examine the interplay of Lawrence's theoretical writings or "metaphysic," especially *Study of Thomas Hardy*, and his art; full, sensitive readings focused on dualism of male and female "principles" in the novels.

Draper, R. P., ed. *D. H. Lawrence: The Critical Heritage*. London: Routledge & Kegan Paul, 1970. Judicious selection of contemporary reviews with helpful commentary.

Edwards, Duane. *"The Rainbow": A Search for New Life*. Boston: Twayne, 1990. A reading that stresses the psychological maturation of Ursula, who has the courage to go beyond consciousness to integrate the unconscious into a new personality.

Farmer, David. "*Women in Love*: A Textual History and Premise for a Critical Edition." In *Editing British and American Literature, 1880–1920*, edited by Eric Domville. New York: Garland, 1976. Detective work on editorial pressures that forced Lawrence to censor himself.

Ford, George. *Double Measure: A Study of the Novels and Stories of D. H. Lawrence*. New York: Holt, Rinehart & Winston, 1965. Wide-ranging study of death and rebirth as theme, including a fine chapter on *Women in Love* as a novel preoccupied with the end of the world.

Gordon, David J. "Sex and Language in D. H. Lawrence." *Twentieth Century*

Literature 27 (Winter 1981):362–75. Some of the complexities in the Lawrentian language of sexuality.

Heilbrun, Carolyn. "Marriage Perceived: English Literature, 1873–1941." In *What Manner of Woman,* edited by Marlene Springer. New York: New York University Press, 1977. Feminist polemic.

Kermode, Frank. *Lawrence.* London: Fontana/Collins, 1973. The interplay of visionary or ideologue and novelist; the testing or "subduing" in the fiction of ideas from prose treatises (e.g., *The Crown* and *Women in Love*); an allegorization of the art.

Kinkead-Weekes, Mark. "The Marble and the Statue: The Exploratory Imagination of D. H. Lawrence." In *Imagined Worlds,* edited by Ian Gregor and Maynard Mack, 371–418. London: Methuen, 1968. Pioneering article on the evolution of Lawrence's vision in "The Sisters" as it can be traced in manuscripts.

Langbaum, Robert. *The Mysteries of Identity: A Theme in Modern Literature.* New York: Oxford University Press, 1977. Lawrence as a writer in the Romantic tradition who explores human identity through sex as Wordsworth explores the human mind through nature; especially good on the animal and mythic in Lawrence's notion of the quintessentially human.

Leavis, F. R. *D. H. Lawrence: Novelist.* Harmondsworth: Penguin, 1964. Classic account of Lawrence as social historian with keen eye for the depredations of class and industry, dramatic poet, and moralist.

Lindsay, Jack. "The Impact of Modernism on Lawrence." In *The Paintings of D. H. Lawrence,* edited by Mervyn Levy. New York: Viking, 1964. Best interpretation of the way Lawrence's empathy with the vision of modern painters (e.g., Futurists, Cézanne) informs his fiction.

Lucente, Gregory. *The Narrative of Realism and Myth: Verga, Lawrence, Faulkner, Pavese.* Baltimore: Johns Hopkins University Press, 1981. The dialectical presence of myth in realistic works; revises notion of Lawrence's career as movement from realistic to mythic.

Meyers, Jeffrey. "Lawrence and Homosexuality." *London Magazine* 13 (1973):68–98. Provocative but reductive; assumes all ambiguity on a complex issue was self-deception.

Oates, Joyce Carol. "Lawrence's Götterdämmerung: The Tragic Vision of *Women in Love.*" *Critical Inquiry* 4 (Spring 1978):559–78. Passionate reappraisal of those elements in the novel that have been dismissed by moralists: Birkin as Hamlet, Gudrun's predicament and Loerke's art; emphasizes tragic at expense of utopian.

Ragussis, Michael. *The Subterfuge of Art: Language and the Romantic Tradition.* Baltimore: Johns Hopkins University Press, 1978. Study of the "untranslatability and intransigent contextuality of words" in the novel, informed by linguistic ideas of Saussure, Merleau-Ponty, and Riffaterre.

Ross, Charles L. *The Composition of "The Rainbow" and "Women in Love": A History*. Charlottesville: University Press of Virginia, 1979. A reconstruction of the history of composition, together with illustrations from the manuscripts and critical discussion of the interpretive uses to which a textual history may be put.

————. "The Revisions of the Second Generation in *The Rainbow*." *Review of English Studies* 27 (August 1976): 277–95. The manuscripts reveal a tension between the chronology in the novel and the chronology of composition; the hostility of the modern world, exposed by the war, was reflected back on the second generation so that the love scenes became a projection of the struggle between primal and social egos.

————. "Homoerotic Feeling in *Women in Love*: Lawrence's 'struggle for verbal consciousness' in the Manuscripts." In *D. H. Lawrence: The Man Who Lived*, edited by R. B. Partlow and Harry T. Moore, 168–82. Carbondale: Southern Illinois University Press, 1980. Revisionist study arguing that Lawrence discovered and controlled his controversial theme in the act of composition and that the final novel is more, not less, candid than "Prologue."

————. "D. H. Lawrence and Greek Tragedy: Euripides and Ritual." *D. H. Lawrence Review* 10 (Spring 1977): 1–19. Lawrence's refashioning of Greek dramatic conventions and scenes in his novels.

Sagar, Keith. *D. H. Lawrence: Life into Art*. Athens: University of Georgia Press, 1985. A genetic study that draws extensively on manuscript drafts.

Simpson, Hilary. *D. H. Lawrence and Feminism*. DeKalb: Northern Illinois University Press, 1982. A chronicle of Lawrence's friendships with activist women and his interest in women's rights and the suffrage movement before the world war.

Torgovnick, Marianna. *The Visual Arts, Pictorialism, and the Novel*. Princeton: Princeton University Press, 1985. Most thorough study of Lawrence's lifelong use of paintings as symbols in his fiction.

Williams, Raymond. *The Country and the City*. Oxford: Oxford University Press, 1973. Humane analysis of Lawrence's "borderline" sensibility and of the inevitable strains in language and sympathy caused by public history and artistic temperament.

Index

Index

The Author

Charles L. Ross received his B.A. from Williams College and his D. Phil. in English literature from Oxford University. He has been awarded Fulbright and Guggenheim fellowships, has taught at the University of Virginia and the University of Hartford, has written *The Composition of "The Rainbow" and "Women in Love": A History,* and has edited a critical edition of *Women in Love.*